Yoga For Profit

D1678018

L. Burke Files

Aegis Journal, LLC.
POB 27314
Tempe, Arizona 85285
Tel (877) 275-4243 - Fax (877) 438-2603

email: Publisher@AegisJournal.com

Sales are available at:

www.AegisJournal.com, Amazon and at Quality Book Stores. Special discounts are available on quantity purchases. Please contact us by email for details. For classroom use, please inquire about the availability of additional support materials.

Orders for bookstores, please contact us by e-mail

Editor: John Conway

Aegis Journal, LLC, the title "Aegis Journal", the Aegis Journal logo, and "How to Start & Maintain a Profitable Yoga Business" are all the property of the Aegis Journal LLC.

To book speaking engagements please contact Mr. Files through Aegis Journal, LLC.

Library of Congress Cataloging-in-Publication Data:

Files, L. Burke
How to Start & Maintain a Profitable Yoga Business

Library of Congress Control Number: 2010903935

Printed in the United States of America

1 3 5 7 9 8 6 4 2

ISBN 978-0-9823723-2-6

I am standing on the road between the Oasis of Bukhara and the Medressehs of Samarkand. A link between provisions for the body and provisions for the mind.

Table of Contents

Preface

My name is L. Burke Files, and I have been an independent business owner since 1982. I also have worked for an investment banking firm that specialized in financing small enterprises and have worked with hundreds of small businesses, helping them get started or assisting them when they got into trouble. One of the businesses I own is Financial Examinations & Evaluations, Inc. www.feeinc.com. As a financial investigator, I really do get to see the worst of the worst, when small businesses are in trouble, and the best of the best, when they are seeking capital for growth.

I have woven into this book the distillation of the experiences (bits of wisdom and folly) that have been harvested from both my experiences as an owner and the experiences of many others that I have pursued or aided.

My Thanks

No book is truly a sole project. It involves many more than the author. I wish to thank Ethan Fialkow for the inspiration, GRL for tons of work, and to John Conway, an editor who is second to none. Many thanks go to everyone at The Aegis Journal, LLC and Financial Examinations & Evaluations, Inc. for your time and support.

Also to my wife Laura and the kids for allowing me the many hours of work, the travel involved, and their enjoyment of the frequent flyer miles.

Introduction

Calm your mind. You've been on a long journey, and you've arrived. Your thoughts are of being independent and helping others. Imagine a turquoise night at a desert oasis. The dry evening air is filled with the faint but familiar sweet smell of spices and water. You watch as new arrivals unpack and relax after their tense travels that brought them to the oasis. Nearby, you watch others pack their goods and wares before steeling for the journey ahead. The time travelers spend at the oasis, between arrival and departure, is time spent contemplating and preparing for the next leg of a journey. It is a time for study, reflection and choice.

Your stay at the oasis will be measured in time spent reading this book, envisioning your future plan, blending a yoga studio, a business and your life. This will be the duration of your stay at the oasis. You've traveled a long distance, but you're ready for what is to come. We plan to make your stay pleasant, informative and authentic so that when you depart, your companion for the remainder of your journey will be the knowledge from the oasis.

Your chosen path leads you to the yoga studio you wish to open. You want it to operate on sound business practices, but reflect your independent style and willingness to help others. It can be all that and more. The burdens that you will bear are all the responsibilities of being an owner, employer and teacher. The joy you will find is in your freedom and financial independence built from a base of solid preparation and wise personal choices.

This is the stream of the oasis, drink from it, rest by it - as others have done yesterday and will do tomorrow.

1 First Challenge

A camel puller is at the head of a file or lian of camels. You don't make money as the puller, but rather from the cargo your animals carry. You do receive wages, but it is from trade that you earn the money to buy more camels. As you progress and buy more camels, you can add them to your lian, compounding the rate of return. When you have a full lian of camels (typically 18) you now pay to join the caravan because you are a partner. You are able to buy the camels because you have practiced the postponement of gratification. You have saved to become an owner. Discipline is required to get you to your goal.

As the owner of a lian of camels, you still do not travel alone. Each caravan has about 18 lian of camels that follow the oldest, wisest leader – the Mister of the caravan. Each lian is paired with a second lian of camels. Together they are called a ba and the camel-pullers of a ba help each other load and unload camels at the beginning and end of the day, as well as with other tasks while on the road. Even though you are the owner, you cannot reach your destination without both the wisdom of those who have traveled before you, and the reliable help of those working with you.

As everyone knows, being a business owner means that you get to work half days – 12 hours. Your pension plan is going to be the value of the business, and you'll be spending more time with your yoga studio, especially during the first stages of the journey, than with your family. You are going to advance from a camel-puller to a Mister – a caravan master – in time, but this is not accomplished from just study and books. You have to make the journey, you need to learn the trade craft.

I have been a self-employed or a commissioned salesperson for all but three years of my adult life. The three years that I spent in a large corporation made an indelible impression on me. I was a rotten employee. If a problem had to be solved, I solved it. If something needed to be done, I did it. I didn't care about areas of responsibility, territory or corporate hierarchy. That attitude didn't go over very well. During this time I took some advice from the second-in-charge of the corporation. He told me, "You need to work for yourself." It wasn't said in a derogatory way, it was said in a friendly and familiar way, from a man who'd been my manager and mentor for those three years. He knew that when he assigned me a task, I didn't argue. I didn't say it couldn't be done. I didn't whine about the resources. I just did it. Looking back, I now know what I didn't know at the time. I wasn't just stepping on toes; I was stepping on whole departments – completely circumventing obstacles (policy and procedure manuals), naysayers and any unwelcomed imposition of authority. Those are the attributes of an entrepreneur, attributes that petrify petty territorial organizations.

Now that you have awoken the entrepreneur inside you, your journey begins. This is a good thing. The independent entrepreneur is the engine of the world's economy. But before we begin, I'd like to comment on nine potential pitfalls that will challenge the budding entrepreneur. You may not face them all, and certainly there are more than nine, but these nine need mentioning.

Time Management: We've all heard the term, and most people plan to look into it someday – when they have the time. To run your own business, you're going to have to invest your time into managing your time. You must clearly understand the difference between productive time, busy time, and family or personal time. You can't spend your entire life with your business – but if you don't manage your time, your entire life may not be enough. Your business will become one of your loves, but it will also be a bitchy, temperamental love. Not at all like the love of friends and family.

There are many good publications on time management, and most are worth reading, but I'm simply going to include a few clues that will let you know when you're getting it right and when you're getting it wrong. You know you're getting it right when the time you spend at the business is productive, enjoyable and building revenue. You are getting time management wrong when you leave at the end of the day and cannot figure out what you've done and are absolutely certain that you need another 10 hours in the day to work on the projects you're leaving behind. If you fail to manage your time, small tasks will waste your day and big tasks will be left undone. If you lose control of your time, you, your friends, and your family will be unfulfilled.

Focus: You have to focus on what's important. You have to make sure that your time is productive and that the time you spend at work moves your business forward according to your plan. One of the oldest and truest expressions in business is "Write a good plan – and work the plan." If you have a good plan, work the plan. You'll never lose your focus or wonder what needs to be done next if you start with a good plan.

One bad plan, if you have a family, is to try and work from home. Early on I started a business working from home, and I found out very quickly that there were 1,000 distractions in the house that I needed to ignore. My office in the home had to become a ritualistic space, a space that could not be violated by children or spouse. It was hard on all of us. I love to have my wife around, and I love to have my children around – but I can't work with constant disruptions competing for my time and diverting my focus.

If there are 1,000 distractions in the house, there are 10,000 distractions outside of your office. As a self-employed entrepreneur, nobody is monitoring your time or following your hours. If you go to lunch and decide to take the afternoon off, there's nobody to scold you. Be careful with your focus, and do not waste your time. Scold yourself when you lose your focus, and put yourself into an environment where there's nobody but you to scold. Excuses on why you cannot get something done means you have failed to take responsibility for your own choices.

Organization: You must organize yourself, your employees, your workspace, your vendors and your customers. They must understand what you expect. You must clearly communicate those expectations and to ensure they are understood. Ask them to repeat your expectations back to you. You must organize those around you so that they don't waste your time, interrupt your focus, or alter the course of your business without your consent. A good business plan, organized filing systems, marketing and accounting systems all contribute to a better use of time and focus.

Fear: Your business can fail. You must understand that. One of the things that you need to do in setting up your business is to set benchmarks of performance. If you aren't meeting your benchmarks, the projections are either unrealistic or you're failing. It's okay to fail. And while I hope it never happens to you, don't become paralyzed by the fear of failure. Opportunity is the assumption of risk. You cannot make a profit without assuming risk. The key to managing risk is to be aware of all of the possible outcomes you are exposed to and being prepared to manage them, hedge them, transfer or bury them. Risk is a desert to be crossed – not all caravans will arrive at their intended destination, and fewer yet with a full load. If you don't understand that, then embarking on the next segment of your journey may be a mistake.

Business Plan: The words "Business Plan" are peppered throughout this text. These words do not refer to your expectations, your wishes, your desires, or your hopes and dreams. A business plan must be written out. It is a projection of future business activity presented as a timeline based upon identifiable assumptions. You must share your business plan with others, such as your attorney and your accountant. Share your business plan with successful entrepreneurs in other fields and they will invariably have insights into costs, services, markets, methods and other assumptions you've made that can help you to move forward. I have found that other business owners are the most generous and authentic resource you will ever find – offering their insights to others who wish to follow in their footsteps to be an independent business owner.

In your business plan, identify your major assets

and resources. These generally include personnel, talent, knowledge, cash equivalents and time. It should demonstrate to the casual reader how you're going to use your cash, time and talent to establish your business, to give your business direction, and to monitor your business's successes and failures. You can only communicate this with a written business plan. I should also mention that no business plan ever survives an encounter with reality. Revise your business plan as often as you recognize that you've made an error in your assumptions – DO NOT revise your assumptions to validate your projections. That is akin to changing the caravan's route to match where you currently find yourself. That would be cheating, and violates the first lesson of the journey, that we must be honest and authentic with every element we include in our plan.

Marketing: Field of Dreams is a lovely film. The premise of the story is "if you build it, they will come." In the real world, nobody really cares what you build. If you want people to come to your yoga studio, you must have a marketing budget and a marketing plan. Marketing is not sales. Marketing is creating an awareness that your business exists, awareness of its products, services and location. The purpose of marketing is to get these messages out to as many potential students as possible – and to as few non-potential students (because it costs money and time). The sale begins when a potential student calls or walks through your door to join your caravan. Marketing gets students to your door.

Sales: Before you've spent all of this money, time and effort on marketing your services, you must have a clear and concise presentation you want to deliver to the people who walk through your door. A clear and concise presentation should lead to a purchase. It should ask them to make a purchase. While it's fine to show off all of your gear, the pleasant ambience of your studio, and your knowledgeable instructors – your objective is to lead them to a purchase. You must ask for the sale.

Technology: Technology constantly changes both the way we do business and what business we do. You must use current technology in every way you can to support your studio. You must stay current on innovations and the evolution of yoga as well as in many fields related to yoga, such as health and nutrition. You need to be savvy with computers, cell phones, PDAs, blogs, POD casts, chat rooms, and be aware of new and emerging technologies that allow you to continue disseminating your message and communicating with your students.

It's all about you: This isn't being self-centered – it really is all about you. If you're not having fun, I can tell you now that your studio is not going to be a fun place, and no one in your family will be having fun. You want to get up every morning knowing what you're doing, knowing what it takes to make you happy, and knowing that your efforts are getting you closer to your goals. If you're not happy at what you're doing, examine what it is that's affecting you. If you can correct it, great – if not, maybe it's time to re-examine your commitment to the studio. Life is too precious to waste time and talents doing something that you are not happy doing. The ambience of your business and your associates' personalities will develop from your lead. Successful journeys are led by knowledgeable, persistent and focused people. These are the people that inspire others to follow them and the caravan.

Shake the date tree and it will drop ripe dates to you. Eat, drink and be at peace.

2 Purpose

The purpose of your yoga studio is to be a profit-making venture and to fulfill your sense of purpose. Profit is not a dirty word. This venture must, above all else, produce a profit (not prophet). It doesn't matter how many accolades, awards or appearances on television you have if you must close your doors. The business journey must also fulfill your sense of purpose. If the journey doesn't fulfill your sense of purpose, you will not want to show up. Neither will your students.

The purpose of your yoga studio is different for your students. They're looking for a better way of life using yoga as a tool. It's a very good tool. The shame is that people often desire good tools, but don't want to pay the price. If you cater to students that want the best instruction for the cheapest price, you will not be happy providing it to them. You will resent the effort and will reduce your effort. The students will sense they are not getting all they can get and will not be happy with the course. If you do not charge enough, they will not respect you – and they will not perceive value in your offering. If you charge enough, you will be happier, the quality of your classes will be better, you will have respect, and your students will perceive value. It is within this balanced environment that your students will sing your praises.

From these short paragraphs I hope you realize that if you don't charge enough, you will not stay in business and your students will not appreciate you. To put it another way, would you choose discount plastic surgery?

Part of your sense of purpose, we can assume, originates from the fact that yoga has had an impact on your life – and you want to share your knowledge and experience in a way that will earn you a living. This sense of purpose is imperative, and you must cultivate it, it is the foundation for your strategies in attracting students to your caravan. Your passion for your mission, your sense of purpose, will get you through the unexpected challenges that will appear in any new start-up enterprise.

Services: What services do you intend to offer? It's a simple question, but not an easy question to answer. You must clearly define all of the services you are going to offer on your first day of business. Your written business plan must also include a clear understanding of what services that you can add as your business matures.

Are you offering classes only? Will your studio sponsor other social events, or organizations, to drive traffic and enhance revenue? Will the center offer merchandise, food, supplements, reading materials or travel opportunities? The services and items you intend to offer need to be crystal clear - not to you but to your prospective and current students. I cannot help but think of the restaurants menus with both descriptions and pictures of the food or windows filled with plastic food on the Ginza. These are simple and comprehensive meal descriptions that educate diners and set their expectations. Be that detailed. The direction you choose, and the complement of services you offer, will drive your marketing efforts.

What services you intend to offer will give you an idea of

the number of square feet you'll need for your business, and direct you toward a location that's conveniently located to your target customer. At this point in our discussion, it's time to design your dream Yoga Center. It's just a design on paper, but it's a beginning. Let's determine in what direction we're headed before we finalize our plans and select a destination for our journey.

The desert is a harsh unrelenting and unforgiving place, but it is part of creation.

3 Facilities

Space is going to be costly. Initially, your rent and related overhead is going to be your biggest expense. Rents and utilities are fixed expenses, it doesn't matter how much revenue you have – you'll have to pay your overhead every month. These expenses don't vary with the quality of service you provide, your number of customers, or your revenue. In a nutshell, once you commit to these expenses you can't lower them – you own them.

When considering a location, you need to look at a number of factors, such as: price, lease terms, access, visibility, utilities, zoning restrictions, landlord restrictions and neighbors. Your base rent is generally expressed in a dollar amount per square foot per year. So a $12 per square foot location would mean $1 per month per square foot. If you're comparing leases, and some of them are listed in dollars per month, convert them to annual dollars per square foot so you can compare costs. You will need to add costs for utilities, water and telecommunications – which will vary between locations. Between locations, you may need to adjust costs to include common area maintenance (CAM), security or parking fees. When you compare one facility against another you can't just look at the cost per square foot, you need to add in all of the things that make the space a usable facility. Only when you have determined the cost of creating a usable space, and amortized that cost over the term of your lease, can you make a comparison based on cost. Total Ownership Cost is the only number that will matter.

Access is important. The location should have plenty

of parking nearby. If you are developing an inner-city facility, look for a location with transit stops nearby.

The facility should be visible, recognizable and easy to find. There is a temptation to make the assumption that good students will make the extra effort to find a good instructor and studio. This leads people to believe that they can choose a hard-to-find (less-expensive) location. I have found this assumption to be almost universally wrong for any business that depends on exposure for revenue. It's also a good tactic to hunt for locations that are near symbiotic businesses, such as well-known supplement retailers, health food stores and gyms.

There are three types of restrictions that may limit your options. The first is zoning, which is fairly straightforward. It means your facility has to be located in an area that allows commercial activity, and has to comply with the rules and regulations of running a yoga studio. The biggest challenge I've seen in the past in this category comes in the form of restrictions that unrealistically limit occupancy. The landlord may also have restrictions that are a part of their standard rental agreement. Some lease restrictions may bar you from conducting your business in the way you're planning. The final hurdle is informal restrictions put on you by your neighbor's expectations. The darn thing is, you'll never know what those expectations are going to be unless you ask everyone in advance, or take a chance of violating their expectations after you move in. Some of the silly things I can envision are a liquor distributor located next to a temperance league, a taxidermist located next to PETA, or an allergist located next to a florist. These are simple and obvious examples and ones I'd like to see. In all likelihood the conflicts will be more subtle and nuanced, and you won't know unless you do some research. You need to introduce yourself, your business model and talk with your prospective neighbors.

Some other things you need to be cognizant of when choosing a location is the development plans for streets in the area, and the status of anchor tenants at this location. If you've just opened up your studio and the city tears up the street limiting access to your location, it is going to affect the business. Even after you open, you must keep appraised of development plans dealing with the access points to your location, and prepare dramatic sales and promotions during the times of disruption to keep cash flowing. The second is thornier, and that is the issue of an anchor tenant. Consider that you've located in a shopping center that has a health food store; it's a wonderful location for you – as long as the health food store remains open. If that business closes, you should have a provision in your lease that provides you the right to terminate your lease without penalty. Another example is a mall with a grocery store, which generally guarantees a lot of traffic. Make your lease contingent on the grocer remaining open. I've seen busy malls turn into ghost towns when an anchor tenant closes – make sure you don't find yourself with a five-year lease in a ghost town.

Here are some other nuggets to consider when selecting a location. Consider what services you're going to need – telephone, Internet, electric, gas, cable, etc. Check with both the telephone company and cable company in your area to find which will provide the most advantageous package for you, and make sure you give them the specific address of the intended studio. Some distances are too far for the telephone company to overcome and offer proper Internet services, other locations simply do not offer cable. Do not assume that you have choices. For gas and electric service, check with the utility company to find out what the bills were for the previous two years at your considered location, this will allow you to compare the total costs of different locations and help develop a more precise business plan. Also, check with service providers for any scheduled rate increases. Check with the police in the neighborhood you're contemplating to see what type of calls for service have occurred in the area – this will help you determine whether you're locating in a high-crime area. If you've only visited the property in daytime, then visit at night – and vice versa. Make sure there's adequate parking and lighting at all times. Do you feel safe at night? Is the parking lot abandoned? Is there loud music and drinking at a neighboring business? Last, but not least, again - go talk to your neighbors. Neighbors are an absolute fountain of information. They probably can tell you, and will tell you, more about the location and the neighborhood than anyone else can.

Assuming you're leasing the space, make sure that you structure your lease for the long-term success of the business. Build in options to extend the lease for long periods of time, and make sure you have sufficient notice from the landlord if he doesn't intend to renew – try to get a one-year notice. I know of a very successful studio that was killed by a landlord. The landlord told the owner, after eight years of leasing, that the lease would only be renewed if they added 5,000 square feet.

The studio was operating in 3,000 square feet, and had no use for the additional space. The studio was forced to move when the entire 8,000 square feet was leased to a restaurant. There was little to no time for relocation plans, and the business died. At least it was a quick death.

Another stupid landlord trick is to rent to one or more businesses that compete with one another – how many stores in the mall need to sell sunglasses before no one can make any money? The same with Yoga – you need to be very clear that when you sign your lease that no competing business will be located in the same complex without your written permission. It would seem logical – but go to a mall and see the problem for yourself.

Some leases require a base rent payment along with a percentage of gross sales over a set cap. This is sometimes a good way to reduce your startup overhead. It allows you to pay additional rent when you can afford it. If you find a lease like this, make sure that everybody has the same understanding of what defines a sale. You may assume that it only includes sales that take place on-site. The landlord may assume that it includes all sales, including Internet sales and revenue from off-site instruction. Both of these are dangerous assumptions. Define the agreement, and make sure to burden all sales in the business plan with their contribution to the rent.

As an alternative to leasing, for a start-up yoga studio, you may consider the option of co-locating. This is where you rent, or co-locate, at a facility being used for another purpose. I have seen yoga studios located with health clubs, dance studios, martial arts studios and adult education centers. I have also seen yoga studios start at community centers, church basements, senior centers and – believe it or not – an airplane hangar. However you choose your location, make sure to understand its strengths and weaknesses as well as its opportunities and risks. A well-thought-out choice, balancing your resources and time, will allow you to confidently move forward with your plan. While there will be many opportunities, only you will recognize the ones that will fit into your future plans.

The oasis lives a precarious existence, one that depends upon protective layers. The most important vegetation is the date palm. It yields high protein fruits and is the first layer of the canopy. Date palms provide the shade for the second layer of trees, usually apricot or peach. Olive trees are grown at the edges of the oasis since they are thick and shield the oasis from some of the winds – they yield fruit and oil. Beneath the trees, vegetables and other delicate crops grow within the protective layers of the oasis. All life depends upon other forms of life, and all life must inhabit the proper location within the oasis in order to thrive.

4 Market

When people have a passion for the services that they intend to provide they assume that they know who their customers are going to be. Never make that assumption. Just like when you're eating a new dish, you take a small bite to test the flavor and texture before committing to a large bite. I must admit, I cherish the memory of the look on a friend's face the time he spread a thick coat of what was thought to be green cream cheese (actually wasabi) on a tuna roll and took a big bite. The added squealing, frantic gestures, color changes and bouncing were pretty funny too. The point is, when you're spending the marketing budget, approach your options cautiously.

An erroneous marketing assumption, consistently made, is that our students will be a lot like us. This is a dangerous assumption because there are so many types of people who are motivated by so many different things. The only way to develop a dependable marketing strategy is to do research.

The first information you want to collect is a local industry profile. Who is currently providing services that are similar or identical to yours? These are the people and their businesses that will be competing with you for students, and you want to know as much about them as possible. Typically, as someone contemplating a new yoga studio, you are aware of many competitors. Learn more, and find out about all of them. Ask as many of your friends and fellow devotees as you can about other studios in the area. At the same time, ask about other interests that they hold, such as martial arts, dancing, theater, dining, shopping, and other places they choose to spend their time and money. You're competing with every other provider of non-essential goods and services for your customer's dollar, so you need to constantly gather information that can be used in future marketing efforts.

Your competition is important because it is likely when you open up your studio that you will be taking students away from these other studios. That's perfectly okay, that's what you want. In fact, you may want to spend some time researching what the students of other studios like and dislike about the studio they attend. This will help you design your studio and know the purchase triggers of the students that attend those studios. Another question that has to be asked is whether the market in the area you want to locate is saturated. If the market is saturated, you're going to have to work extremely hard at both developing new students and converting students of other studios to attend your location. Generally when a market is saturated, you'll recognize it by extreme price slashing. If your studio doesn't have any significant differentiating features from your competitors in town – find some. Your customers must have a reason and find the motivation to change their current habits.

Physically, where are your customers located? In New York City it is unlikely that a student will commute seven miles to a studio. This is because, at different times of the day, a seven-mile commute may take more than an hour. This isn't true in a city such as Phoenix, Arizona, where a seven-mile commute, even in the worst of traffic, is 10 to 20 minutes or less. The critical issue in determining your marketing area is not the physical distance as much as it is the length of time the student will need to commute between home and your studio. This is another question you should ask your friends and contemporaries – how long, in time, do they currently travel to attend their yoga studio, how long are they willing to travel to attend a yoga studio?

Consider the socioeconomic status of each of your students. Here, you can basically create two groups. In the first group we have students who will come to your studio for classes. The second group is composed of those you will visit at their homes or offices for more personal or intimate group instruction.

You should now have an idea of who your potential students are, and after talking to your contemporaries and fellow devotees you have some knowledge of where they spend their time. Using this information you should have some ideas about where and how you can get your name in front of potential students.

What is your message? What do you want potential students to know about yoga, and in particular, about you and your studio? You can't communicate this entire message in a flier, and you can't fit it into a simple advertisement. The only way you can properly communicate this is in person. So, as you create awareness about yourself and your studio you must concurrently create the opportunity for people to visit your studio. Either get them to come through your door, or find an opportunity for you to go through their door. Your message must be clear and must differentiate you from your competition. Your message doesn't have to be original, it has to be effective.

I remember working with a studio owner whose

business had fallen on hard times. He had highly skilled and knowledgeable instructors. No one there could understand why their marketing materials, which worked well for 18 of their 25 years in business, had suddenly failed. The owner of this studio, I found out in conversations with him, was the original instructor in town and had trained the instructors at most all of the competing studios. The owner had not only taught the students well, but had filled them with the passion to open their own studios. Our plan was to change the marketing approach and update the interior of the studio. In a dramatic fashion, we announced to the entire community that the studio would be closed 30 days for a stunning transformation. The studio's windows were papered over with brown craft paper, and we only allowed the workers to enter. Nobody passing by knew what was going on inside. At the same time we redeveloped the marketing plan, especially the message. Five days before opening, the marketing plan was unveiled to everyone in town. Every competitor who at one time had trained for the studio owner was invited to bring their students to the master for advanced training. It was understood that the trainers would receive some compensation, both financially and in advanced training for the participation of themselves and their students. At the same time a postcard was sent to every former and current student inviting each one of them back for the opening night festivities – "to celebrate with the master who had trained the trainers." Opening night was marvelous. The event was catered by several talented experts, at their cost, which allowed the local artisan chefs to display their skills. Entire cases of new merchandise and training materials were there for everyone to see and buy, all located in a beautifully redecorated modern studio.

From opening night through the first week, the trainer who trained the trainers quadrupled business at the studio. This was accomplished by understanding the studio owner's strength – which was that he had trained the competing trainers. This created an opportunity to offer the students of his students specifically advanced training. He went from being just another instructor to the instructor.

Branding: This is the process of creating a message and an image in both a potential customer and current client's mind that not only accurately describes their expectations in consuming your services but anything else upon which you use your brand. It is an implied process to the consumer of the level of quality, knowledge and value that they can ascribe to anything carrying your brand. An attractive brand name draws others to you and a strong brand will produce much higher returns that a bland brand. Create your brand and defend it from competitors, derogatory remarks and slipshod suppliers.

Do not be surprised if you fall each day, do not give up. Stand your ground courageously.

5 Business Structures

Your business structure is the legal form under which you conduct business with your students and suppliers, and under which you will enter your contractual relationships. This list is at best only a general guideline. You need to speak with your legal and accounting professionals to obtain the best advice for your personal situation.

Sole Proprietorship: This is the most common legal business form. In fact, most businesses start out as a sole proprietorship. In this simple structure, you, the entrepreneur, are the owner of all of the assets – and exposed to all of the liabilities of the business. Within the limits of the law, you are in complete control and can make choices about the business as you see fit.

Profits of a sole proprietorship flow directly to personal income and are generally reported for tax purposes on you 1040 Schedule C. The proper gain or loss from business activity is then reported on Form 1040. You are also expected to file Form1040 ES, along with Form 4562, which covers depreciation and amortization of assets, employment tax forms if you have employees, and Form 8829 if you use your home for business purposes. Shortcomings of a sole proprietorship include the deductibility of some expenses, in particular medical insurance, as well as some difficulty in raising capital.

Federal tax forms for a sole proprietorship (a partial list, and some may not apply)
- Form 1040: Individual Income Tax Return

- Schedule C: Profit or Loss from Business (or Schedule C-EZ)
- Schedule SE: Self-Employment Tax
- Form 1040-ES: Estimated Tax for Individuals
- Form 4562: Depreciation and Amortization
- Form 8829: Expenses for Business Use of your Home
- Employment Tax Forms

If this sounds a little daunting – relax. It's not really that complicated. Make sure to add an accountant to your list of expenses when developing a business plan.

Partnerships: Partnership structures are an option when two or more people own and control the business. General partners in a general partnership are responsible for the day-to-day activities, management of the business, and are generally liable for all of the debts and obligations of the partnership. Limited partnerships protect passive investors, and their liability to the partnership is specifically set forth in the partnership agreement, which generally limits their liability to a contractual amount. Partnerships are relatively easy to establish, but you must be prepared to invest in the professional time, energy, and legal effort to create the partnership agreement. The agreement sets forth how you intend to run the partnership and how you intend to deal with serious disagreements and dissolution. Off-the-shelf partnership agreements will not suit your needs. The appropriate use of such form agreements is to get you thinking about the needs, rights and constraints you want in the final agreement

– but they are not the customized documents you want for a final agreement. The profits and losses from a partnership flow directly through to the partner's personal tax returns.

The ability to raise funds is generally enhanced when compared with a sole proprietorship. One disadvantage is that general partners are jointly and collectively liable for the actions of the other general partners. As choices about a business's future are shared, there will eventually be disagreements.

Federal tax forms for a general partnership (a partial list, and some may not apply)

- Form 1065: Partnership Return of Income
- Form 1065 K-1: Partner's Share of Income, Credit and Deductions
- Form 4562: Depreciation
- Form 1040: Individual Income Tax Return
- Schedule E: Supplemental Income and Loss
- Schedule SE: Self-Employment Tax
- Form 1040-ES: Estimated Tax for Individuals
- Employment Tax Forms

Corporations: Corporations charters are issued/ granted by a state. It may or may not be the state in which you are located. If it is not the state where you are doing business, you will have to domesticate the corporation in the state where you are doing business. The corporation is a unique legal entity, and a barrier to many types of liability – meaning that shareholders may be protected from many types of liability that a business can be exposed to. A corporation that is legally constructed and properly operated should prevent claims from flowing through to the shareholders. The owners of a corporation, the shareholders, control the corporation by electing a board of directors to oversee the major policies and choices of the corporation. The board of directors hires senior management and directs them as to how the company is to be run. One of the advantages of a corporation is that the shareholders have limited liability for corporate debts. Generally, shareholders can only be held accountable for the purchase price of the shares. Corporations can raise additional funds through the sale of stock, but must be careful not to run afoul of state or federal securities laws. A corporation may also elect to structure itself as an S corporation if certain requirements are met. This option enables the corporation to be taxed similarly to a partnership. One note on liability – while liability may not flow through to shareholders, officers and directors can be held liable for their actions, such as the failure to withhold tax payments with the consequence of misrepresenting the corporate status to a third party. A corporation requires a little bit more time and money to establish than other forms of business structures. Corporations are monitored by federal, state and local agencies, and almost always have more paperwork to process. Incorporation usually results in higher overall taxes because the earnings are paid out in dividends after the federal government taxes the earnings, and dividends are then taxed when received by the shareholders, unless you have elected an "S" corporation. In a small corporation with few shareholders who all work for the company, this double tax can usually be managed by authorizing the payment of bonuses. Also understand that as a small corporation many lenders, landlords and creditors will ask for, or require personal guarantees for all contracts.

Federal tax forms for regular or "C" corporations (only a partial list and some may not apply)

- Form 1120 or 1120-A: Corporation Income Tax Return
- Form 1120-W Estimated Tax for Corporation
- Form 8109-B Deposit Coupon
- Form 4625 Depreciation
- Employment Tax Forms
- Other forms as needed for capital gains, sale of assets, alternative minimum tax, etc.

Subchapter S corporations refer to a tax election choice for the corporation made with the IRS, not to the incorporation process of the entity. Subchapter S status is not determined at the time of incorporation but rather at the time you apply for your taxpayer identification number from the IRS. The catch here is that if the shareholder is working for the company, and if there is a profit, the shareholder must pay himself a reasonable compensation for his work. A person working for a corporation, owning the corporation, and receiving dividends but no wages is simply waving a red flag in front of the IRS.

Federal tax forms for subchapter S corporations (only a partial list and some may not apply)

- Form 1120S: Income Tax Return for S Corporation
- Form 1120S Schedule K-1: Shareholder's Share of Income, Credit and Deductions
- Form 4625 Depreciation
- Employment Tax Forms
- Form 1040: Individual Income Tax Return

- Schedule E: Supplemental Income and Loss
- Schedule SE: Self-Employment Tax
- Form 1040-ES: Estimated Tax for Individuals
- Other forms as needed for capital gains, sale of assets, alternative minimum tax, etc.

Limited Liability Companies (LLC): Limited Liability Companies represent a relatively new hybrid business structure and are permissible in most states. They are designed to provide the limited liability features of a corporation along with the tax efficiencies and operational flexibility of a partnership. Its formation is more complex than for a general partnership. The ownership of the LLC are the members. Management of the LLC can be vested in the members where it is a member-managed LLC or can be vested in a manager where it is a manager-managed LLC. The members and managers can be persons, corporations, partnerships, or trust foundations – it doesn't matter. The unit of ownership in an LLC is a membership unit. The duration of the LLC is finite and its date of termination /windup is disclosed with the organizational papers at the time they are filed. Although the termination/ windup limit can be continued if desired, the LLC must not have more than two of the four characteristics that define corporations: limited liability to the extent of assets, continuity of life, centralization of management, and free transferability of ownership interests.

The tax forms for LLC will be either corporate tax forms or partnership tax forms, depending upon the tax election taken at the time of formation.

Special Forms of Structures: There are also specialty structures for companies in some states.

The Limited Liability Partnership, or LLP, is organized to protect individual partners from personal liability for their negligent acts or acts of other partners or employees not under their direct control. This structure is not recognized by every state, but the common restrictions include that the LLP must provide a professional service such as medicine or law for which each partner is licensed.

A Professional Service Corporation (PSC) must be organized for the sole purpose of providing a professional service for which each shareholder is licensed. The advantage is limited liability for the shareholders. This is an option available to certain professionals such as doctors, lawyers and accountants. You will need to check with your state to find out which occupations qualify.

A Limited Partnership is typically a more complex formation and requires at least one general partner who is fully responsible for the partnership's obligations and normal business operations. A limited partner is often an investor who is not involved in the day-to-day operations. This structure shields such investors from liability beyond the amount of their investment. The limited partners do not pay tax, but must file a return for informational purposes and pass, on a pro rata basis, a share of profits and losses to the partners via K-1.

Nonprofit Corporations are typically formed for civic, educational, charitable and religious purposes. This structure enjoys tax-exempt status and limited personal liability. Nonprofit corporations are managed by a board of directors, or trustees, and assets must be transferred to another nonprofit group if the corporation is dissolved. Being chartered as a nonprofit doesn't mean you don't owe taxes, just that the accumulation of donations and assets are exempt from taxation as long as the nonprofit status is maintained. UBIT - Unrelated Business Income Tax may be assessed if there is commercial activity that does not substantially relate to the non-profits core functions. Nonprofit status is elected at the time of formation with the state, and requested from the IRS. Nonprofit status is not always granted.

A roof rests upon the walls.
The walls rest upon the foundation.
The walls and roof enclose the home.

A wall rests upon the foundation.
The foundation rests upon the earth.
The earth is what we are made of and will return to.

6 Accounting Considerations

Once you've chosen your form of business you must secure an EIN – or Employer Identification Number. An EIN is requested from the IRS and can be done online. An EIN is a TIN (Tax Identification Number) for a business just as a Social Security number is for a person.

You also have to select an accounting method. The two acceptable methods are cash basis and accrual basis.

The cash method of accounting records the cash flow of financial events when they occur. This method recognizes revenues when cash is received and recognizes expenses when cash is paid out. In cash accounting, revenues and expenses are also called cash receipts and cash payments. The cash method of accounting does not recognize promises to pay, either from the business or from the business's clients. When the cash method of accounting is elected, it is also used when reporting to the IRS.

The accrual method of accounting records all economic activities and financial events of the business. According to this method, revenues and expenses are recognized whether or not they have been received or paid. The accrual basis of accounting is the most accurate if you require an economic snapshot of a business or need to compare business activity between different periods. Accrual accounting is required for all public companies.

The accrual basis of accounting tends to be more costly to maintain properly, because it requires a bookkeeper to record many more transactions as well as to identify and recognize transactions that are contracted to occur (or not occur) at some date in the future.

Accrual is the better form for accounting, as it's more authentic and informative. However, typically I suggest that small businesses use the cash basis of accounting and that they only switch to accrual before they intend to sell the business, or when the business has grown to a sufficient size that the accrual method is required for proper planning. Be aware that if you elect to operate your business using the cash method, you can elect to switch to accrual at a later date – you cannot switch from accrual to cash.

If there's going to be more than one owner in a business, I cannot stress enough the involvement of an attorney to draft the formation documents. You will require the firm's services to prepare the proper articles and bylaws for corporations or member and management agreements for LLCs, as well as to formulate a buyout agreement. Not only will you need some professional advice on how to deal with other owners, but also there will come a day when an owner needs to sell. Sometimes it's not a choice to sell, but rather normal events of life that force a sale. For example: The shares of your corporation that belong to your investor are now in the hands of a bankruptcy trustee, and the bankruptcy judge sees a need to liquidate the shares and/or the business to satisfy creditors. Another possibility, more common, is the untimely death of a partner or shareholder whereupon the shares are passed to heirs, and the heirs want to sell. The small amount of time and money required to properly prepare a business structure is cheap insurance and should provide you some comfort as you go forward. Keep in mind that any issues that are not identified and dealt with in the foundational documents will need to be dealt with in arbitration or litigation.

I fully admit that none of this is any fun. I get it. Preparation for a journey is tedious, but so important. Loosely tied cargo is lost and insufficient water will spell doom. Our time spent here at the oasis, in this book, is not the fun element in the spice-charged and perfume-filled air of entrepreneurship, it is the drudgery of preparing for the journey. Yet its value rises during the journey. You must not leave the oasis with insufficient food, water, equipment or beasts of burden.

The dogs may bark but the caravan moves on.

7 Beginning the Business Plan

In my last search of Google I found 26 million sites offering information about how to write a business plan. I'm going to try and simplify it for you, as it's really not that complicated.

Creating a business plan is like creating a detailed income and expense summary before the fact. You're visualizing the journey of the caravan. Let's say we're creating a business plan for our first year in business. Our plan details every revenue category, along with the amount of revenue expected from each source during the year. Our plan also includes every expense category along with the amount we expect to pay during the year. In this hypothetical one year plan, all we have to do is subtract our total expenses from our total revenues to determine our profit (or loss).

Now let's introduce our plan to reality. We open our business, follow the plan, and then we tabulate our actual revenues and expenses after one year of operation. If the business plan was perfect, the two documents should be identical. They never are. You will never see a perfect business plan, you will see some very good plans.

Chances are your plan was very close in estimating the annual expense for things like rent, utilities, memberships and dues. These expenses are determined by contract, or can easily be researched. But your plan probably entirely missed some expense categories that you became aware of during the year, such as a broken air conditioner that, after re-reading your lease, you discovered was your responsibility. You may have found that you needed to make some changes to the building that required extensive electrical, plumbing and carpentry work that wasn't in your budget. A municipal sign ordinance may require you to hire an approved contractor that you didn't anticipate. There are a number of unanticipated expenses you may encounter. This is where good research and experience help. And that's just the expense side of the ledger. If we compare the revenue side of our business plan to actual revenues one year later, there's a high probability that we've missed some categories here as well, but it's more likely that we projected the source of income or the rate of revenue growth incorrectly.

Our plan has one other problem. We calculated revenues and expenses for our first year, but we didn't calculate how those revenues and expenses were distributed during the year. We need more information. For example, a lot of our expenses will probably fall in the first month or two as we outfit the studio and make a lot of long-term purchases. On the other hand, the bulk of our revenue will probably be realized in the later months of the year, with the revenue increasing as our enterprise matures. This presents us with a problem, because we need to know how much money we're going to require to implement our plan. The plan is going to need more detail, so what we do is create a financial outlook for every month of the year. By charting months, we can see exactly how many months will pass before we expect to be profitable, and how much money we expect to spend before we expect to be self-sufficient (if not profitable).

Our challenge is to create an outlook of financial statements for a business that isn't even open yet. How do we design a business plan that we can believe in? We include as much information about our foreseeable needs, and we do as much research as possible. And, as we stated earlier, we show our plan to other business people and professionals. Spreadsheet programs such as Microsoft Excel or Open Office Calc have made this process so much easier than it was in the past, that I wouldn't even consider starting the process without spreadsheet software. If you don't know how to use spreadsheet software – and even if creating this one business plan is the only time you will ever use it – believe me it will be well worth your time to learn.

If you don't have a copy of Microsoft Excel, you can download Open Office from www.openoffice.org. It's free, and almost identical to Office. It's just as functional.

Caravan Yoga Studio – 1st Year Projections

Assumptions	
Number of square feet	1,500
Cost per square foot	12.75
Utilities per 100 ft2	40.50
Cost per Month - Group	89.00
Cost per Private Session	100.00
Insurance Monthly	155.00

Employees / Marketing / Maintenance	
Counter Help - Monthly	2,100
Instructor - Monthly	2,700
Students per Instructor	80
Organic Growth Mo.	15%
New Students from Mktg Mo.	5
Equip Maint % Monthly	5%

One Time Expenses	
Property Improvements	11,250
Equipment Purchases	8,500
Grand Opening Budget	2,500

Month	0	1	2	3	4	5	6	7	8	9	10	11	12
Expense													
Rent	1,594	1,594	1,594	1,594	1,594	1,594	1,594	1,594	1,594	1,594	1,594	1,594	1,594
Utilities	608	608	608	608	608	608	608	608	608	608	608	608	608
Insurance	725	155	155	155	155	155	155	155	155	155	155	155	155
Internet / Phone Mo.	110	110	110	110	110	110	110	110	110	110	110	110	110
Advertising		250	250	250	250	250	250	250	250	250	250	250	250
Counter Help	2,100	2,100	2,100	2,100	2,100	2,100	2,100	2,100	2,100	2,100	2,100	2,100	2,100
Instructor #1	2,700	2,700	2,700	2,700	2,700	2,700	2,700	2,700	2,700	2,700	2,700	2,700	2,700
Instructor #2	0	0	0	2,700	2,700	2,700	2,700	2,700	2,700	2,700	2,700	2,700	2,700
Instructor #3	0	0	0	0	0	0	0	2,700	2,700	2,700	2,700	2,700	2,700
Instructor #4	0	0	0	0	0	0	0	0	0	2,700	2,700	2,700	2,700
One Time Expenses	22,250												
Equip Maintenance		425	425	425	425	425	425	425	425	425	425	425	425
Total Expense	30,086	7,941	7,941	10,641	10,641	10,641	10,641	13,341	13,341	16,041	16,041	16,041	16,041
Cumulative Expense	30,086	38,028	45,969	56,610	67,251	77,893	88,534	101,875	115,216	131,258	147,299	163,340	179,381

Revenue

	0	1	2	3	4	5	6	7	8	9	10	11	12
Student Membership	**45**	45	57	70	86	104	124	148	175	206	242	284	331
Private Classes	**12**	12	14	16	18	21	24	28	32	37	42	49	56
Students - Group		4,005	5,051	6,253	7,636	9,227	11,056	13,159	15,578	18,360	21,559	25,238	29,468
Private Classes		1,200	1,380	1,587	1,825	2,099	2,414	2,776	3,192	3,671	4,221	4,855	5,583
Food Service													
Garments		250	288	331	380	437	503	578	665	765	879	1,011	1,163
Studio Rental		400											
Total Revenue	0	5,855	6,718	8,171	9,842	11,763	13,972	16,513	19,435	22,795	26,660	31,104	36,214
Cumulative Revenue	0	5,855	12,573	20,744	30,586	42,349	56,321	72,834	92,269	115,065	141,724	172,828	209,042
Cumulative Net Profit	-30,086	-32,173	-33,396	-35,866	-36,665	-35,544	-32,213	-29,041	-22,947	-16,193	-5,574	9,488	29,661

43

The Caravan Yoga Studio's 1st Year Projections are a sample of a very simple business cash flow plan created in Excel. If you would like to download the file to see how it is formatted or to use it as a template, it can be downloaded from www.yogaforprofit.com by clicking on the link.

I'm guessing these assumptions and calculations need some explaining. First of all, a business plan has to answer several very basic questions, such as:

- Is the proposed venture profitable?
- How much money will I need?
- If I borrow the money, when can I pay it back?
- Is the venture realistic?

In order to answer these questions, we have to start making some assumptions. You'll notice on the top of the business plan is a section conveniently titled "Assumptions," which are broken into three columns. As the assumptions are set forth, you'll see how the narrative of the business plan begins to grow. If you're trying to borrow money to pursue your plan, you'll be asked to, and should be able to, defend every number you present. Here's how to read your business cash flow plan, starting with the first column:

> Number of Square Feet. From our research, after investigating several properties, we plug in the one we like, which is 1,500 square feet. We estimate that the maximum number of students at a location this size could handle about 300, each coming in twice a week for a two-hour session.

Cost per Square Foot. We enter in the rental rate. If the rate is a flat monthly rate, convert its cost per square foot per year so that you can easily compare all rates.

Utilities per 100 Square Feet. With a single call to the local electrical provider, we were able to find out the average monthly rate in that building per 100 square feet. Most utility companies have plans that allow you to pay a flat rate year-round to avoid seasonal fluctuations, which is what we entered in here. This is probably a safe number to use in the plan, but we bumped it up a couple dollars per 100 square feet just to be safe. In reality, we'll probably have higher air conditioning costs in the summer because of the number of bodies in the rooms – but we'll have lower heating costs in the winter for the same reason. Try to get the average electrical use for the building you intend to occupy, not an average for per 100 square feet for the city – all buildings are not equally efficient.

Cost per Month. We intend to provide multiple classes for members who will pay a membership fee of $89 per month for unlimited use. This number comes from our research of competitors and interviews with students. We feel that this is the right offering at this time in this location.

Cost per Private Session. We are currently providing private lessons for $100 per session at the client's location. We intend to continue this practice, so this is a second revenue source.

Insurance Monthly. We're working with a single agent who has combined all of our insurance needs into a single policy. We've provided the agent with the details of this location and he has quoted us a premium.

The next column of assumptions covers employees, marketing and maintenance.

Counter Help. We have found an employee we want to work the front counter, answer phones and help with sales. She has asked for $10 an hour. We have developed a relationship with a payroll service named XYZ Pay. We pay the service 20% above the actual payroll, and it provides all of the payroll services, including the payment of all payroll taxes. We calculated this by first multiplying the number of weeks in a month by the 40-hour workweek we expect the counterwoman to work.

52 / 12	= 4.33 weeks in a month
4.33 x 40	= 173.3 hours per month
173.3 x $10	= $1,733.00 employee earnings
$1,733 x .2	= $346.60 payroll and payroll taxes
$1,733 + $346.60	= $2,079.60

The next step was simply to round up to $2,100. If there's a chance your numbers may be a little off – always round expenses UP, and round revenues DOWN. It is always best to overestimate the distance being traveled, and underestimate the amount of help you receive along the way. Not dramatically, just enough to

46

give you a small cushion.

Instructor. From our research and interviews of several qualified instructors in the area, we found that we would be able to have our choice of instructors if we paid $17.00 an hour – so that's the figure we used. We expect them to be working about 30 hours per week. Other than that, we simply calculated our cost using the formula on the previous page.

Students per Instructor. In our research of class sizes and services currently being provided, we calculated that we would be able to provide a far superior service if we limited the number of students an instructor taught within a week to 80. In our business plan, the spreadsheet adds a new instructor every time the number of students increases by 80. If we lower this number in our assumptions, the additional instructors will impact the budget at an earlier date – increasing our cost. If we raise this number, additional instructors will come on the payroll at a later date – decreasing our cost.

This is not a number we recommend for you. You're going to have to defend the numbers you arrive at from your research. This is going to involve gathering information from other studios in your market, and determining the level of service you intend to provide.

Organic Growth. There are several factors that help an enterprise grow, but organic growth is the most elusive, and most important. This is growth that's due to word of mouth, goodwill, signage, and people simply stumbling upon your operation. It includes current students bringing friends and neighbors, and other informal methods of getting people through your doors. We have estimated organic growth to be 15% per month.

You must be aware that there is a saturation point for organic growth. You can have a faster growth rate, but it's not going to be organic growth. You must set a reasonable limit to govern this type of growth, as it cannot continue indefinitely. As an example, if you own the only Chinese restaurant in a town of 10,000 people, and you know that 50% of the population likes to go out for Chinese food once a month, there's a strong chance that market will find you. That market represents your limit for organic growth.

You can safely assume that 5% of the population served by your studio either practice or have practiced Yoga in some form. Consider that portion of the population to be the limit for the organic growth of all studios serving that population.

New Students from Marketing. Another way to grow the enterprise is by advertising. The growth from advertising will be fundamentally different than organic growth. An effective advertising campaign will show a somewhat linear relationship between dollars spent and results. Here, we are estimating that we can gain five new students a month from our advertising budget. Our entire advertising budget currently is spent advertising on the receipts and placemats of a health food restaurant next door to our preferred location.

Equipment Maintenance. We've calculated the maintenance on our equipment as a percentage of the total cost. Using a 5% monthly figure, we can completely update our equipment every 20 months. While this may seem aggressive, we estimate that we may want to experiment with some new equipment, so we have made sure the budget will allow us to do so. Old or worn equipment is very bad for your image, make sure you've budgeted enough.

The next section of assumptions has to do with fixed costs. These are expenses that we don't expect to ever have to make again.

Property Improvements. We had a contractor come to the site to give us a quote for the work we wanted to have done. His quote was $11,250. This number should be supported by another tab, or worksheet, on the spreadsheet that details the work to be done, the terms, and the estimate or quote as well as contact information for the contractor. It's important that you use the spreadsheet as a tool to store all of the information you collect – because you will eventually find yourself revising and making both major and minor changes to the business plan to make it work. As a note, when you hire contractors make sure you have a set date for completion and that there are financial penalties for failing to complete the work by the agreed upon date. If not, the work will drag on and on and will be done at the contractor's schedule and not yours.

Equipment Purchases. We have studied the equipment being used at other studios in the area, and talked with other students. We have decided that we will provide equipment that will be the best in the market. We requested quotes from several suppliers and have chosen the best, which is $8,500.

Grand Opening Budget. We plan to open the studio with a party, catered by the health food restaurant next door to us. (Our cost is for food only.) We have been given a price for music by a string quartet popular in town, and we plan to do advertising targeted to the neighborhood. We have a $2,500 budget. This expense really should be detailed on another tab of the workbook.

Reviewing the Business Plan

So now that you have a short narrative covering most of the assumptions – let's look at how the plan is developed from those assumptions. Notice that there are columns numbered 0-12 under the assumptions section. These columns represent the time it takes to prepare your business to open, along with the first 12 months of operation. Column 0 represents expenses you have prior to opening. Columns 1-12 represent your first year of operation. This plan assumes that it will take one month or less to prepare the studio for opening, and that revenue will begin in the first month.

In column 0, we have added some line-item assumptions. These numbers are in bold, and represent some known costs, and some one-time fees. In column 0 under insurance we put $725 to cover the first month's premium that includes one-time fees to initiate the policy. In the expense category Internet-phone we put a monthly fee of $110 representing a quote we received from the telephone company for our data and voice lines.

In column 0, under the revenue heading, we indicated that we currently have 45 students. These are students who we currently teach at other locations and have indicated they will stay with us in our new location. We've also listed the 12 private classes we teach, because we don't expect any changes. These are existing sources of revenue.

Notice that under the expense section there are two rows with the headings "Total Expense" and "Cumulative Expense." There are two similar rows under the revenue section. These represent the ongoing expenses and revenues of the studio. On the bottom line is the cumulative net profit – revenue less expense. Now let's use the plan to answer the questions we posed earlier in this chapter.

Is the proposed venture profitable? If our assumptions are correct, yes it is. According to the plan, the studio shows an operating profit in the fifth month, when revenues of $11,763 exceed expenses of $10,641. But in the fifth month, as you can see on the bottom line, you're still out-of-pocket $35,544. You don't get your initial investment back until the 11th month, where the plan shows a profit of $9,488.

You may have noticed that, in this plan, the owner is not being paid. If the owner or a manager requires a salary, that will push these dates out further.

How much money will I need? According to the plan, the most money ever invested into the studio is in the fourth month. On the bottom line you can see a cumulative loss of $36,665. According to the plan, if all of our assumptions are correct, you won't need more than $37,000. Be very careful about how you interpret this number. If any of our assumptions are wrong, such as our estimate of the growth rate, the operating profit may be delayed by several months. You don't want to set aside $37,000 just to see the doors locked and the power shut off in your studio when an additional $5,000 would have seen you through that period. You need reserves, and you need sources you can depend on if you need to buy time. Whatever amount the business plan requires, I would want to have about 125% of that on-hand, and another 20%-30% in available credit if I need it. For this plan, I would want to have about $47,000 on-hand, $10,000 in available credit, and living expenses for more than a year.

Most people have to make some changes in their personal life before starting a business. You must prepare for medical or family emergencies, and other unforeseen events that could cause a business interruption. Any such interruption is going to affect the financial requirements. Many of these can be covered by insurance, so you should address any concerns you have with your agent.

If I borrow the money, when can I pay it back? This is tricky. According to the plan, the maximum investment is in the fourth month, with the business showing a loss of $36,665. There is an operating profit beginning in the fifth month, and by the 11th month the venture is profitable. According to the plan, you could borrow $37,000, completely pay it back between months 5-11, and begin realizing an income of more than $20,000 a month by the end of the first year. If you, in actuality, structure a loan to be repaid by the end of the year, you are leaving yourself very little room for error. I would want as much time as the lender was willing to give me. You can always pay a loan early, paying late has severe consequences. If you're borrowing money, make sure you share your forecasts with the lender, listen to any suggestions they offer, and make sure to keep your lender up to date on your progress.

A common solution is called pass-through lending. In this system, the lender provides excess capital to the debtor so the debtor can make interest-only payments until the venture is cash-flow positive. It increases the overall debt burden quite a bit, but it provides you with an example of some of the solutions lenders will consider.

Is the venture realistic? Let's look at a few of our assumptions and see how they have ramped up over the timeline we created. This is the time to do a reality check. If we go through the process correctly, not inflating our projected revenues or underestimating our expenses, the process will be self-correcting.

Notice that under the heading of revenue I have two rows that represent the number of projected members, and the number of private classes that will be taught. The numbers 45 and 12 represent existing students – so those numbers are okay. Next, let's look at how these numbers ramp up over time. By month 12 we project to have 331 dues-paying members and 56 private classes monthly. Are these numbers realistic? Probably not in a town of 10,000 – but we're convinced that we can reach them in our hypothetical market. We've determined how many students are currently in town, and calculated that this would only represent 5% of the existing market. That seems reasonable. Looking through our plan, we can rethink some of our assumptions. Assume we have reservations about the rate of growth, so we decide to reduce the organic growth rate to 10%. It's a low rate of growth – but it's safer.

Our next question is, will the facilities support more than 300 members? When we started, we were thinking of 300 students coming twice a week for two hours. Now we're already over 300 in the first year, with no place to grow. And we have to consider the drop-in traffic. We're beginning to think that 1,500 square feet is going to be a little cramped – so we're going to try a neighboring facility that is 2,500 square feet. The larger site allows us to continue growing.

The nice thing about working with a spreadsheet is all I have to do is type in these two changes, and my projections for my business plan are instantly recalculated. With these changes, the plan begins showing an operating profit in month seven, but doesn't show profit in the first year, so I extend the plan another year simply by copying the formulas in column 12 and pasting them into 12 new columns, 13 to 24, representing the second year. I also added rows for new instructors, allowing the plan to grow into the second year.

2,500 Square Feet with a 10% Growth Rate

The new plan, printed on the following pages, shows an operating profit in the seventh month, and shows a net profit in the 15th month. The greatest investment came in the sixth month, with a total of $45,983. In the 15th month we have 311 students, projected gross revenue of $33,164 and expenses of $20,209, leaving a profit of $12,955.

In the 16th month we have 347 students, projected gross revenue of $36,926 and expenses of $20,209, leaving a profit of $16,717.

In reality, I would stop the growth in this plan at about the 15th or 16th month because that's probably all the facility can handle. At that point, the business is profitable, and the owner(s) will have $10,000-$15,000 a month in continuing profit. This is a plan we can work with.

For this plan I need $45,983, but I want to have about $60,000 (±1.25%), a reserve of available credit around $15,000, and $75,000 for one-and-a-half years of living expenses.

Caravan Yoga Studio – 1st Year Spreadsheet

Assumptions		Employees / Marketing / Maintenance		One Time Expenses	
Number of square feet	2,500	Counter Help - Monthly	2,100	Property Improvements	11,250
Cost per square foot	12.75	Instructor - Monthly	2,700	Equipment Purchases	8,500
Utilities per 100 ft2	40.50	Students per Instructor	80	Grand Opening Budget	2,500
Cost per Month - Group	89.00	Organic Growth Mo.	10%		
Cost per Private Session	100.00	New Students from Mktg Mo.	5		
Insurance Monthly	155.00	Equip Maint % Monthly	5%		

Month	0	1	2	3	4	5	6	7	8	9	10	11	12
Expense													
Rent	2,656	2,656	2,656	2,656	2,656	2,656	2,656	2,656	2,656	2,656	2,656	2,656	2,656
Utilities	1,013	1,013	1,013	1,013	1,013	1,013	1,013	1,013	1,013	1,013	1,013	1,013	1,013
Insurance	725	155	155	155	155	155	155	155	155	155	155	155	155
Internet / Phone Mo.	110	110	110	110	110	110	110	110	110	110	110	110	110
Advertising		250	250	250	250	250	250	250	250	250	250	250	250
Counter Help	2,100	2,100	2,100	2,100	2,100	2,100	2,100	2,100	2,100	2,100	2,100	2,100	2,100
Instructor #1	2,700	2,700	2,700	2,700	2,700	2,700	2,700	2,700	2,700	2,700	2,700	2,700	2,700
Instructor #2	0	0	0	0	2,700	2,700	2,700	2,700	2,700	2,700	2,700	2,700	2,700
Instructor #3	0	0	0	0	0	0	0	0	0	2,700	2,700	2,700	2,700
Instructor #4	0	0	0	0	0	0	0	0	0	0	0	0	2,700
Instructor #5	0	0	0	0	0	0	0	0	0	0	0	0	0
Instructor #6	0	0	0	0	0	0	0	0	0	0	0	0	0
Instructor #7	0	0	0	0	0	0	0	0	0	0	0	0	0
Instructor #8	0	0	0	0	0	0	0	0	0	0	0	0	0
One Time Expenses	22,250												
Equip Maintenance		425	425	425	425	425	425	425	425	425	425	425	425
Total Expense	31,554	9,409	9,409	9,409	12,109	12,109	12,109	12,109	12,109	14,809	14,809	14,809	17,509
Cumulative Expense	31,554	40,963	50,371	59,780	71,889	83,998	96,106	108,215	120,324	135,133	149,941	164,750	182,259

Revenue

	0	1	2	3	4	5	6	7	8	9	10	11	12
Student Membership	**45**	45	55	65	76	89	103	118	135	154	174	196	221
Private Classes	**12**	12	13	15	16	18	19	21	23	26	28	31	34
Students - Group		4,005	4,851	5,781	6,804	7,929	9,167	10,529	12,026	13,674	15,486	17,480	19,673
Private Classes		1,200	1,320	1,452	1,597	1,757	1,933	2,126	2,338	2,572	2,830	3,112	3,424
Food Service													
Garments		250	275	303	333	366	403	443	487	536	589	648	713
Studio Rental		400											
Total Revenue	0	5,855	6,446	7,535	8,734	10,052	11,502	13,097	14,852	16,782	18,905	21,241	23,810
Cumulative Revenue	0	5,855	12,301	19,836	28,569	38,621	50,123	63,220	78,072	94,855	113,760	135,001	158,811
Cumulative Net Profit	-31,554	-35,108	-38,071	-39,944	-43,320	-45,376	-45,983	-44,995	-42,251	-40,278	-36,181	-29,749	-23,447

Expense	13	14	15	16	17	18	19	20	21	22	23	24
Rent	2,656	2,656	2,656	2,656	2,656	2,656	2,656	2,656	2,656	2,656	2,656	2,656
Utilities	1,013	1,013	1,013	1,013	1,013	1,013	1,013	1,013	1,013	1,013	1,013	1,013
Insurance	155	155	155	155	155	155	155	155	155	155	155	155
Internet / Phone Mo.	110	110	110	110	110	110	110	110	110	110	110	110
Advertising	250	250	250	250	250	250	250	250	250	250	250	250
Counter Help	2,100	2,100	2,100	2,100	2,100	2,100	2,100	2,100	2,100	2,100	2,100	2,100
Instructor #1	2,700	2,700	2,700	2,700	2,700	2,700	2,700	2,700	2,700	2,700	2,700	2,700
Instructor #2	2,700	2,700	2,700	2,700	2,700	2,700	2,700	2,700	2,700	2,700	2,700	2,700
Instructor #3	2,700	2,700	2,700	2,700	2,700	2,700	2,700	2,700	2,700	2,700	2,700	2,700
Instructor #4	2,700	2,700	2,700	2,700	2,700	2,700	2,700	2,700	2,700	2,700	2,700	2,700
Instructor #5	0	0	2,700	2,700	2,700	2,700	2,700	2,700	2,700	2,700	2,700	2,700
Instructor #6	0	0	0	0	2,700	2,700	2,700	2,700	2,700	2,700	2,700	2,700
Instructor #7	0	0	0	0	0	2,700	2,700	2,700	2,700	2,700	2,700	2,700
One Time Expenses								2,700	2,700	2,700	2,700	2,700
Equip Maintenance	425	425	425	425	425	425	425	425	425	425	425	425
Total Expense	17,509	17,509	20,209	20,209	22,909	25,609	25,609	28,309	28,309	28,309	28,309	28,309
Cumulative Expense	199,768	217,276	237,485	257,694	280,603	306,211	331,820	360,129	388,438	416,746	445,055	473,364

Revenue	13	14	15	16	17	18	19	20	21	22	23	24
Student Membership	248	278	311	347	387	430	478	531	589	653	723	801
Private Classes	38	41	46	50	55	61	67	73	81	89	98	107
Students - Group	22,085	24,739	27,658	30,869	34,400	38,286	42,559	47,260	52,431	58,119	64,376	71,259
Private Classes	3,766	4,143	4,557	5,013	5,514	6,065	6,672	7,339	8,073	8,880	9,768	10,745
Food Service												
Garments												
Studio Rental	785	863	949	1,044	1,149	1,264	1,390	1,529	1,682	1,850	2,035	2,239
Total Revenue	26,636	29,745	33,164	36,926	41,063	45,615	50,621	56,128	62,186	68,849	76,179	84,242
Cumulative Revenue	185,447	215,192	248,356	285,282	326,345	371,960	422,581	478,709	540,895	609,744	685,924	770,166
Cumulative Net Profit	-14,320	-2,084	10,871	27,588	45,743	65,749	90,761	118,580	152,457	192,998	240,869	296,802

Business Plan Meets Reality

Let's follow our hypothetical caravan as it advances into the reality of the desert.

The first thing I did, which was recommended earlier, is to visit my attorney. My attorney advised me that the name of my studio, YogaForProfit, should be trademarked – add $4,000. I needed a business transaction permit if I wanted to sell merchandise – add $60. When I signed the lease with the landlord, they required three months rent paid in advance to originate the lease – add $5,312. When I had the power turned on, the utility service required a deposit – add $2,000. The signage I had intended to display was not approved by the city. I was required to use one of three approved sign companies servicing the complex I was in. I took the lowest bid – add $3,200.

When I finally began moving into the studio space, I realized there were no hand towels, no toilet paper – nothing. What was I thinking? This studio is intended to support more than 300 students. Most of the studio is carpeted, but the reception area is tile. After moving things in and organizing, it already needed some touch-up. I didn't have a vacuum or a tile cleaner. The windows needed cleaning. The room I had set aside as the employees lounge didn't have anything in it – I needed a refrigerator, microwave, coffee maker, cups, napkins, plastic ware, paper products ... all of those things I took for granted. I began making a list. My first trip was to WalMart – add $5,700.

The contractor came to begin construction on the changes we had agreed upon. He asked if I had the building permit. No. Add $200 and a two-day delay. Once the refrigerator and microwave were placed in the lounge area, we found that between some combination of the microwave, the refrigerator cycle, and the normal load, we frequently tripped the circuit breaker. That circuit included the lobby lights and front-counter computer. This happened quite frequently, so we finally called in an electrician to split the circuit and add a new breaker – add $750.

Communication systems became more important as we were completing the studio. While we were building it, we relied on our individual cell phones and the single business line at the front counter. As we got closer to completion we realized the need for an internal phone system that allowed us to transfer calls, to conference call, and to provide voice mail – add $1,250 using the existing wiring.

I went to my graphic designer and Internet expert to explain some of the changes I would need to implement the sign-up, registration and scheduling features on the studio's Web site. She needed $4,300 for the design and programming as well as $250 to set up the card-processing account with the bank.

I then began receiving requests from suppliers that I send them order confirmations on our company letterhead. We didn't have any letterhead. I also found out that many of our students would not be able to pay by automatic debit – they required a mailed invoice. I then scouted out a friendly printer who informed (reminded) me that I would need business cards, letterhead, envelopes, remittance envelopes, cash receipts and other stationary items. Cost for printing and office supplies, $2,200. Cost for graphic design, $450.

In frustration I finally went to my accountant to regroup. He told me I needed to buy a copy of Quick Books, $500, plus training for three people, $2,100. Accountant, $700.

This is all *before* opening. Here are the cost totals I forgot to include:

Trademark	$ 4,000
Sales Tax Permit	60
Lease Deposit	5,312
Power Deposit	2,000
Signage	3,200
Outfit Office	5,700
Building Permit	200
Electrician	750
Phones	1,250
Internet Programming	4,300
Card Processing	250
Printing and Supplies	2,200
Graphic Design	450
Quick Books	500
Training	2,100
Accountant	700
Total	$ 32,972

So, the unaccounted-for pre-opening expenses total $32,972. This is over and above the pre-opening expenses anticipated in the business plan of $31,554. This means that the pre-opening costs are 104% over budget. Clearly this needs to be addressed.

In reality, most of these additional expenses could have been and should have been anticipated. The only item that could not have been anticipated is the $750 for the electrician – but even here, the budget for the remodel project should have anticipated some miscellaneous expenses to cover unexpected costs.

Trying to include everything into a business plan is a lot of work. You really need to go look at facilities that are similar to what you intend to build, and look around. Yoga and dance studios are a good place to start. Computers, desks and chairs are obvious – but things like staplers, pens, stationary, copy paper, postage, software, artwork, fax machines, printers and cables are not as obvious. The little things really add up. To keep your plan organized, create separate worksheets that group miscellaneous expenses and then put a single line on the business plan referencing that worksheet. This makes the plan much easier to read, because you can simply view the worksheet referenced in the line item for details. For the list above, I created a worksheet called "Misc_Opening," created a new worksheet titled Plan No. 3, added a row under expenses called "Miscellaneous Opening Expense," and populated month 0 with the total from the new worksheet. What we now have is a business plan that includes all of these expenses that should have been anticipated.

How do we know, even with these new expenses added, that we've accounted for everything we're going to need? We don't. We spend as much time as is practical to determine what our costs are going to be. We call for prices, we make notes of everything we learn, we round prices up, and we're still going to be wrong. So, we add one more line to our expense section, and we call it "Other Stuff." I look down to my expense total, and I add about 25% of the total for miscalculations. This is after I've made a detailed list.

This new plan, printed on the following pages, still shows an operating profit in the seventh month, but doesn't show a net profit until the 18th month. The greatest investment came in the sixth month, with a total of $94,606. In the 15th month we have 311 students, projected gross revenue of $33,164 and expenses of $20,209, leaving a profit of $12,955. In the 16th month we have 347 students, projected gross revenue of $36,926 and expenses of $20,209, leaving a profit of $16,717. In reality, I would consider stopping the growth in this plan at about the 15th or 16th month, because that's about all the facility could handle. At that point, the business is profitable, and the owner(s) will have $10,000-$15,000 a month in continuing profit. This is a plan we can work with.

For this plan I need $94,606, but I want to have about $120,000 (±1.25%), a reserve of available credit around $30,000, and $75,000 for one-and-a-half years of personal living expenses. Total required before committing to the plan, $225,000.

Notice that in the original plan, we were considering going forward with a total of $75,000 for the business, and $75,000 for personal living expenses. From the following plan you can see that we would have spent our entire budget, including reserves, and dipped into our living expenses for a little more than $5,000 before even opening. By the end of the sixth month, the business would have dipped into the living-expense budget by $19,606. In those six months, presumably we would have personally used up one-third of our living expenses, or $25,000. This would have left us with a total of $30,394 for both business and personal expenses at the end of the sixth month. Seeing that this latest plan doesn't generate a net profit until the 18th month, there's only $30,394 to survive for one year. At the end of the sixth month the owner would have to begin making some lifestyle changes, or be prepared to go on the payroll and delay the break-even point even further.

From this analysis, even our first plan may have survived. It would depend upon the owner's risk tolerance. But the plan *could* survive only because we had set aside one-and-a-half years of personal expenses. If the owner had proceeded with only the $60,000 estimated cost and $15,000 reserve, it would have failed spectacularly. You can't depend upon your business to support you until it matures, and that may be longer than you think.

Assumptions

Assumptions	
Number of square feet	2,500
Cost per square foot	12.75
Utilities per 100 ft2	40.50
Cost per Month - Group	89.00
Cost per Private Session	100.00
Insurance Monthly	155.00

Employees / Marketing / Maintenance

Employees / Marketing / Maintenance	
Counter Help - Monthly	2,100
Instructor - Monthly	2,700
Students per Instructor	80
Organic Growth Mo.	10%
New Students from Mktg Mo.	5
Equip Maint % Monthly	5%

One Time Expenses

One Time Expenses	
Property Improvements	11,250
Equipment Purchases	8,500
Grand Opening Budget	2,500
Utility Deposit	2,000

Expense

Month	0	1	2	3	4	5	6	7	8	9	10	11	12
Rent	7,969	2,656	2,656	2,656	2,656	2,656	2,656	2,656	2,656	2,656	2,656	2,656	2,656
Utilities	1,013	1,013	1,013	1,013	1,013	1,013	1,013	1,013	1,013	1,013	1,013	1,013	1,013
Insurance	725	155	155	155	155	155	155	155	155	155	155	155	155
Internet / Phone Mo.	110	110	110	110	110	110	110	110	110	110	110	110	110
Advertising		250	250	250	250	250	250	250	250	250	250	250	250
Counter Help	2,100	2,100	2,100	2,100	2,100	2,100	2,100	2,100	2,100	2,100	2,100	2,100	2,100
Instructor #1	2,700	2,700	2,700	2,700	2,700	2,700	2,700	2,700	2,700	2,700	2,700	2,700	2,700
Instructor #2	0	0	0	0	2,700	2,700	2,700	2,700	2,700	2,700	2,700	2,700	2,700
Instructor #3	0	0	0	0	0	0	0	0	0	2,700	2,700	2,700	2,700
Instructor #4	0	0	0	0	0	0	0	0	0	0	0	0	2,700
Instructor #5	0	0	0	0	0	0	0	0	0	0	0	0	0
Instructor #6	0	0	0	0	0	0	0	0	0	0	0	0	0
Instructor #7	0	0	0	0	0	0	0	0	0	0	0	0	0
Instructor #8	0	0	0	0	0	0	0	0	0	0	0	0	0
Legal and Accounting	5,000												
One Time Expenses	24,250												
Misc Opening Expense	20,310												
Other Stuff	16,000												
Equip Maintenance		425	425	425	425	425	425	425	425	425	425	425	425
Total Expense	80,176	9,409	9,409	9,409	12,109	12,109	12,109	12,109	12,109	14,809	14,809	14,809	17,509
Cumulative Expense	80,176	89,585	98,994	108,403	120,511	132,620	144,729	156,838	168,946	183,755	198,564	213,373	230,881

Revenue

	0	1	2	3	4	5	6	7	8	9	10	11	12
Student Membership	**45**	45	55	65	76	89	103	118	135	154	174	196	221
Private Classes	**12**	12	13	15	16	18	19	21	23	26	28	31	34
Students - Group		4,005	4,851	5,781	6,804	7,929	9,167	10,529	12,026	13,674	15,486	17,480	19,673
Private Classes		1,200	1,320	1,452	1,597	1,757	1,933	2,126	2,338	2,572	2,830	3,112	3,424
Food Service													
Garments		250	275	303	333	366	403	443	487	536	589	648	713
Studio Rental		400											
Total Revenue	0	5,855	6,446	7,535	8,734	10,052	11,502	13,097	14,852	16,782	18,905	21,241	23,810
Cumulative Revenue	0	5,855	12,301	19,836	28,569	38,621	50,123	63,220	78,072	94,855	113,760	135,001	158,811
Cumulative Net Profit	-80,176	-83,730	-86,693	-88,567	-91,942	-93,999	-94,606	-93,617	-90,874	-88,900	-84,804	-78,371	-72,070

67

Expense	13	14	15	16	17	18	19	20	21	22	23	24
Rent	2,656	2,656	2,656	2,656	2,656	2,656	2,656	2,656	2,656	2,656	2,656	2,656
Utilities	1,013	1,013	1,013	1,013	1,013	1,013	1,013	1,013	1,013	1,013	1,013	1,013
Insurance	155	155	155	155	155	155	155	155	155	155	155	155
Internet / Phone Mo.	110	110	110	110	110	110	110	110	110	110	110	110
Advertising	250	250	250	250	250	250	250	250	250	250	250	250
Counter Help	2,100	2,100	2,100	2,100	2,100	2,100	2,100	2,100	2,100	2,100	2,100	2,100
Instructor #1	2,700	2,700	2,700	2,700	2,700	2,700	2,700	2,700	2,700	2,700	2,700	2,700
Instructor #2	2,700	2,700	2,700	2,700	2,700	2,700	2,700	2,700	2,700	2,700	2,700	2,700
Instructor #3	2,700	2,700	2,700	2,700	2,700	2,700	2,700	2,700	2,700	2,700	2,700	2,700
Instructor #4	2,700	2,700	2,700	2,700	2,700	2,700	2,700	2,700	2,700	2,700	2,700	2,700
Instructor #5	2,700	2,700	2,700	2,700	2,700	2,700	2,700	2,700	2,700	2,700	2,700	2,700
Instructor #6	0	0	2,700	2,700	2,700	2,700	2,700	2,700	2,700	2,700	2,700	2,700
Instructor #7	0	0	0	0	2,700	2,700	2,700	2,700	2,700	2,700	2,700	2,700
Instructor #8	0	0	0	0	0	0	0	2,700	2,700	2,700	2,700	2,700
One Time Expenses												
Misc Opening Expense												
Other Stuff												
Equip Maintenance	425	425	425	425	425	425	425	425	425	425	425	425
Total Expense	17,509	17,509	20,209	20,209	22,909	25,609	25,609	28,309	28,309	28,309	28,309	28,309
Cumulative Expense	248,390	265,899	286,108	306,316	329,225	354,834	380,443	408,751	437,060	465,369	493,678	521,986

68

Revenue	13	14	15	16	17	18	19	20	21	22	23	24
Student Membership	248	278	311	347	387	430	478	531	589	653	723	801
Private Classes	38	41	46	50	55	61	67	73	81	89	98	107
Students - Group	22,085	24,739	27,658	30,869	34,400	38,286	42,559	47,260	52,431	58,119	64,376	71,259
Private Classes	3,766	4,143	4,557	5,013	5,514	6,065	6,672	7,339	8,073	8,880	9,768	10,745
Food Service												
Garments	785	863	949	1,044	1,149	1,264	1,390	1,529	1,682	1,850	2,035	2,239
Studio Rental												
Total Revenue	26,636	29,745	33,164	36,926	41,063	45,615	50,621	56,128	62,186	68,849	76,179	84,242
Cumulative Revenue	185,447	215,192	248,356	285,282	326,345	371,960	422,581	478,709	540,895	609,744	685,924	770,166
Cumulative Net Profit	-62,943	-50,707	-37,751	-21,034	-2,880	17,126	42,138	69,958	103,835	144,375	192,246	248,180

Always keep in mind that the majority of new businesses fail. It's really no mystery that most fail – and it's no mystery that only a few succeed. The difference is in the owner's knowledge, expectations and research. It can all be seen in the owner's planning or lack of planning. Your well-written, well-researched realistic business plan will be your road map to success.

My experience working with business startups covers more than 25 years. In that time I've identified several types of business owners. There are a few types that are almost guaranteed to fail, the two that stand out are: Imperial Potentate and Business Slave.

The Imperial Potentate will order the caravan into the desert and command it to arrive at its destination. The Imperial Potentate always believes they see the big picture, and consequently does little research. Why do research when you already know the answer? This type listens to very few people, if any at all, and they rest on their royal laurels. When failures occur, it's always somebody else's fault.

The Business Slave is doing everything: buying supplies, watering and loading the camels planning the route, protecting the caravan from raiders, monitoring the weather and adjusting the route. The business slave is over tasked. They try to do everything, thus few things are done well. To the business slave, all failures are the will of the gods.

Well-balanced caravan leaders understand their responsibilities. They work to their strengths, and they staff to their weaknesses. They always listen to other views, and they make choices cautiously. They accept responsibility, learn from their mistakes, and if they choose wrong, they correct it as soon as possible and choose again. A well-balanced leader will cultivate loyalty, respect, and lead the caravan to its destination almost every time.

Recognize our failability as humans as they pour from us when we are tired and we girt them when we are invigorated.

8 Managing the Center

Personnel. Note that in our business plan we begin operation with two employees, one whose title is counter help, and one who is an instructor. Add yourself, and that makes a staff of three. Any staff this small is going to be a fairly casual group, with everybody taking a role in all aspects of the business. The only role that's clearly defined is that of instructor, but as you get your business started there isn't going to be enough work for a full-time instructor. This means you're going to have to utilize the time of all your employees, as well as your own time, in the best way possible to move your plan forward. Make sure employees understand your expectations when you hire them. In a small business, everyone has to promote, sell, schedule and clean. You don't want to hire the proverbial maid who doesn't do windows. Everybody will be expected to wear many hats, do janitorial work and do windows. As you add employees there will naturally be more specialization.

Your choice to add an employee to your payroll is one of the most pivotal choices you will ever make in defining the success of your enterprise. Just as an employee can be a rewarding and profitable addition to your future plans, he can be a destructive and costly detraction. Your choice to hire, and whom you choose to hire, can literally mean the difference between your success and failure. The qualities you're looking for are somewhat obvious, but they're also difficult to find. First, the applicant needs to be qualified to perform their job, and that determination is left to you. Do not underestimate the need for qualifications and experience, because from your customer's viewpoint, the people working at your studio are the studio. You'll want to begin the process of hiring by networking, telling everyone you know that you're looking for help, and what qualifications you need.

By the way, people lie. People never lie more fully and convincingly as when it brings them an advantage. People are never better than when they are on paper and all of their references are friends or relatives. The cost of a background check and aggressive vetting of their credentials and claims is strongly recommended. Be authentic, and tell all applicants that you: 1) perform background checks, and 2) are very thorough in researching and testing their credentials and abilities. Anybody who is insulted or outraged by your statements is already caught and eliminated.

You may need to advertise to get your help-wanted message out. I would suggest staying away from newspapers, as they are becoming less effective and more expensive by the year. Look for local online job bulletin boards, use Craigslist (www.craigslist. com), and use the free throwaway publications found in most cities. Use the telephone to screen callers for qualifications, make sure they know where you're located, what hours they would be expected to work, what their duties would be, and what the compensation range is. Don't waste time talking to people who don't have the qualities you want. Only set up in-person interviews with people who have convinced you on the phone that they have a chance of being hired.

Once you are comfortable with the qualifications of an applicant, you're ready to move on. Let's go through the process. Let's say you set up an interview with four qualified candidates, and you meet with each of them at separate times. After the interviews, you've eliminated one candidate simply because your personalities clashed and you didn't like them. That's a perfectly valid choice to make, because you're going to be spending a lot of time with the person you hire. While "likeability" is a valid factor in eliminating a candidate, do not make the mistake of simply hiring the applicant you like the best. Likeability is a valid reason on its own to include in hiring criteria – but it's not a good reason to hire on its own. There are many other factors to consider once you've pared this list down to three qualified applicants. When you meet for a personal interview pay close attention to little things, and make notes:

- We re they on time?
- Did they bring a resume, or ask for an application? (Have some on hand.)
- What was their appearance? Will they fit in with the business culture?
- Do they speak well?
- How much different is the experience of meeting them vs. talking to them?
- If you pause the conversation, will they pick it back up?
- Did they provide both work and personal references with names and numbers?
- Did they provide home, cell and e-mail contact information?
- Did they arrive by car? Does their transportation look reliable?

These are all little things you need to note along with your overall impression of their personality, people skills and initiative to sell themselves as an employee.

Don't ever hire somebody in the interview or before you've met with all of the qualified applicants, because you're not done yet. Make preliminary choices while you're interviewing, but all applicants' references still need to be checked. One warning here, I've met a lot of thieves and chronic liars, people who will make your life a living hell if they get too deep inside your organization. They all have one trait in common – they're the nicest people you will ever meet. They are nothing like your annoying relatives.

Next, you need to consider the relative qualifications and resumes of the applicants. Chances are, you've already made a choice about whom you would like to hire – but you simply don't know enough about him yet. You need to call their previous employers and personal references. When you call previous employers, always try to talk to the applicant's past supervisor. You will find that many employers are unwilling to talk with you because of liability issues. One safe question, that will tell you a lot, is whether this person would be eligible for rehire? Remember that the applicant is giving you safe references. The "employer" may actually be their wife or brother. They may have omitted several jobs they were fired from. Is there continuity in their employment history? Verify the dates of employment with their previous employer, not by giving them the dates on the application but by asking them to give you the dates this employee worked for them. Is this a real employer? Check the phone number using an Internet search engine – ask them if they have a Web page. Handle the personal references in the same way. Ask how long they've known the applicant, and compare it to the applicant's statement. People will forget dates of hire, and how long they've known their friends – but the references should come pretty close to what is on the application.

If the provided references for your first choice of applicants check out, you should go one step further. You should be able to find a private investigator to do a background check for about $200. This is very inexpensive insurance when you consider the cost of having to terminate an employee and rehire. Most private investigators have access to databases that will fairly reliably tell you if this person has ever been arrested, involved in civil disputes or litigation, been in prison or filed bankruptcy. While all of this information may not be available in your state, a private investigator will proceed following your state's guidelines. Not all information is available in all states for all reasons. This is information you want to know. While something like a previous arrest for marijuana or a DUI may not cause you to change your mind – you really do want to talk about it with the applicant, let them know you're aware of a problem in the past, and let them know that drug use will not be tolerated on company time. You're in charge; you can interpret all of the information you collect in any way you want. It's your enterprise, and you can do as you please. One simple piece of advice that I can provide is, people rarely change. If you're thinking of hiring somebody who has had drug problems in the past, chances are good there will be drug problems in their future. If you really want them, make as a condition of hire, a drug screening program. If you're thinking of hiring someone who has had theft problems in their past, try to eliminate all opportunity for employee theft. Just keep in mind that there are hundreds of ways for an unethical person to take money from your enterprise.

They can game the workers compensation, disability or unemployment programs. They can reallocate your assets, or use your facilities off hours and sell your customer list. There is really no end to the number of creative ways that people lacking in ethics can take advantage of a trust relationship. If you have any reservations, you should land on the side of caution. Remember that your staff is there because they bring some expertise and they can perform a function – don't get too caught up in a personality that appeals to you. By the way all employees are replaceable, even you.

After you've made your choice, you call the applicant and tell them that you would like to work with them. Don't tell them that they "have the job." Remember, they're going through the same process as you are. You've looked at several applicants, and they've probably submitted applications for several positions. They may already be employed, are looking at other offers, or have changed their mind after looking at other opportunities. This is your chance to sense their commitment and enthusiasm for the position you're offering. It's also a time to make sure everybody is on the same page and understands the compensation arrangements, benefits, holidays, hours and responsibilities. Assuming everyone is in agreement, you create an employment agreement, which summarizes your shared understanding. At this point in your relationship it's unlikely that you're creating an agreement that guarantees employment for any period of time or discusses severance. What you may discuss in this agreement is an understanding that you intend to address these issues at a future date, say, three to six months after employment. This probationary period will allow you to judge your new hire's attitude, appearance, knowledge, and other skills you require of them for your survival.

It's a good idea to prepare an employee manual summarizing all of your policies and expectations. A comprehensive manual will prevent any misunderstandings that may arise in the future if terminations are challenged or discrimination is charged. You can find templates for employee manuals on the Internet, which you can copy, edit and shape to suit your needs. The employee manual should address all understandings you have with your employees, and be updated whenever policy changes. You should retain a signed copy from each employee stating that they have read and understand the policies contained in the manual.

Keep in mind that an employee manual should not define any job positions too narrowly, should be compliant with all state labor laws, and should represent a set of rules that you can live with (on the presumption that you will probably be the first to violate them). Have the manual reviewed by competent labor counsel.

The Front Desk and Counter. The front desk is the heart of your operation. You want to greet people who walk in immediately. Your students have made a sacrifice in time and money to show up at your studio, and they should get a warm and fuzzy feeling when they walk in. In this position you want someone who is good at small talk, but not gossip. They need to be exceptionally pleasant, but not patronizing. They need all of the qualities of a good salesperson, along with the qualities of a great administrator. This is a multi-tasking position, handling sales, tours, scheduling, information requests, phones, computers, billing, collections, customer service and any number of other tasks. In this position, you must put your best foot forward. You must make sure that everyone in the studio knows how to help out in this position, but you should make the front counter one person's responsibility and one person's space.

This welcoming feeling that you're trying to create requires an effort to control the ambience of the studio. Everything from decorating, lighting, design, and even odor should be controlled. I recommend some sort of uniform for the staff. If you have shirts with your company logo that you intend to sell from the studio, pick out one color that's for the staff only, and have their names embroidered on the shirts or name tags made. Use a warm color for the staff uniforms, as well as a color that blends well with the decor. You may want to use different colors for different positions. The point I hope to make is that appearances are very important. All staff should be clean, well-groomed, and keep a neat work area – and uniforms are a great way to control appearances.

Suppliers. With most of your suppliers, unless you have an established relationship, you're going to start out working on a cash basis. You should still request an open account with all of your suppliers, and submit a credit application. When you have established open credit with a supplier, most of them will invoice based on a 30-day net payment. On 30-day invoices, ask if they offer discount terms for payment in five days. Many suppliers will offer discounts that are usually 1-2%. In many cases, discount terms are better than cash terms. The secret here is to always take the discounts –

a 2% discount for a net 5 day payment is earning 104% on your money! Quick pay makes quick friends, who in turn will provide preferential treatment.

If your suppliers accept payments by credit card, always request a discount of at least 2% for cash payments. The 2% discount is what they would have to pay for processing a credit card, so there's no loss to the supplier and most will give it. Let your suppliers know that you accept invoices by FAX or e-mail, which if they are set up to do so speeds up their accounting and saves them money.

Wisdom emerges from experience. Experience is gained through the saturation of actual deeds. Deeds are done when the tongue is silent.

9 Operations

Accounting. Accounting is a significant aspect of your operations, and it's a function that you, as an owner, should control until your studio matures. It's important that you have hands-on experience and knowledge of all financial matters, so I would suggest that as the owner, you place all orders and pay all bills. Keep these records locked up.

One exception to this is payroll. Unless you have experience and are comfortable with payroll taxes and forms, you should use an outside service. For a payroll service you can expect to pay a total of $3 to $5 per check issued, which includes the fees for quarterly filing. If you've ever done a payroll, you'll understand the value of this service.

Keep all records, for both revenue and payments. Since you're using the company checkbook for all payments, you can simply store receipts in a chronological file. Receipts are simply supporting documents that you'll need in the event of an audit. Assuming that you have filed and paid all of your taxes, keep business records for at least four years from the date of payment. It may also be worthwhile to invest in a document scanner to ensure that no records are lost or altered.

Insurance and Liability. Each instructor working with you must carry their own professional liability insurance, and the studio should have a commercial general liability policy that also covers product liability and personal injury. The yoga community has a number of professional associations that have structured low-cost plans that will fit most needs. A simple Internet search will produce several associations providing yoga insurance. If you are currently a member of any professional yoga association, chances are you will find that it has an affiliated insurance provider. Your state, city, county and possibly your landlord may require other insurance. Make sure the requirement for instructors to carry private professional liability insurance is a part of your employment manual, and make sure you verify that they have current policies. Have the instructor cause the insurance company to have you and your studio as an additional loss payee. Make a copy of the employee insurance policies or cards and keep them in the permanent records of the company.

Miscellaneous. We assume that with your experience and knowledge, having been around yoga studios, that you have a well-rounded knowledge of what needs to be done and who will be doing it. We also assume that not all of you have been as closely acquainted with the business side of the operation, so we're going to cover a few of the policies and forms that need to be considered.

Prospecting. There are many good software packages available that will make your sales and follow-up procedures more accurate and efficient. Generally known as contact management software, I've used several. My favorites are Act and Goldmine. Both programs are good, and both have many more features than most people will ever need. There are new software programs entering the field every time I check, so do a little research on price and features. There is robust competition between online providers, which offer browser based contact management. While these services require that you have an active Internet connection to access your data – many of them are free for a single user with a limited number of contacts. I have been satisfied with all of the offerings I've tried, and would pay special attention to pricing in making another choice.

No-Shows or Cancellations. No matter how diligently you make and confirm appointments, some people will simply not call you, and not show up. No call - no show. You will get as many excuses as you would from a second-grader trying to explain 30 missing cookies. The most effective policy I have seen is a three-tiered approach. Your first reaction should be concern – call to see if they're all right. The second reaction is forgiveness, and the third is a polite statement of your policy. The fourth no-show should be a billable event. Applied over six months or so, this policy should take care of people whose conflicts are costing you time and money.

Renewals. Your best prospects are always your current clients, and you want to ensure that they continue as customers. You need to begin the renewal process 30 to 45 days in advance of an annual contract's expiration date, and at least a week in advance of a monthly contract or trial membership. If you can get people to sign up for automatic renewals, offer them a financial incentive. Automatic renewals will save you money and make you money.

Guest Register. All guests should sign in and provide valid identification. You want to try to capture their contact information for phone, mail and e-mail. One method I like is a duplicate book of guest passes. As the guest fills in their information, a copy is made for your records. The best method I've seen however, was a touch screen that the guest used to enter their information. The system printed a pass and receipt for the guest. This same system was used for members to login with their password or membership card. This type of automated data collection works as sweetly as anything I've ever seen.

Membership Contracts. In an ideal world we wouldn't require contracts. But our journey is about reality. Contracts set forth expectations and obligations that both parties to the agreement understand and accept. I could offer you sample contracts for membership, but you will be better served by finding a contract being used in the area you plan to open as a beginning for your own. Whatever agreement you choose to use, make certain it's simply written, uses clear language, and has been reviewed by a contract attorney licensed in your state.

Programmed Tours. When you have visitors, have them login as guests and offer them a programmed tour of the facility. Do not allow haphazard tours. You should have a scripted, mapped tour of the facility answering all of the questions a client is likely to have along the way. The tour should have different scripts for those new to yoga and those with experience looking to expand their horizons.

A Calendar of Tasks. There are certain functions that have their own rhythm. Day and night, weekly and monthly, semiannual and annual rhythms. Define those items as they arise and chart them for each month on a calendar. This can be done with a computer program or with a good old-fashioned hard copy. The message here is that if you have it charted and on the calendar it is likely you will not forget them. Examples are: membership renewals, rent payments, insurance payments, license renewals, vacations, promotions, seasonal events that require advanced planning, cleaning jobs, changing air filters, vacuuming (daily), rest rooms (daily), windows (weekly), et cetera.

The Sale of Services. Customers buy based upon an expectation of value, and re-buy based upon the fulfillment of those expectations. It's that simple, and that complex. Selling services is unlike selling a physical product. Each individual buyer of a service has their own expectations, and may not be able to vocalize them or even understand them. You have to work with your prospective clients and ask them questions to clarify both of your expectations. If you can fulfill the client's needs and wants – tell him and show him. Then ask for the sale.

> *"Mr. Tetley, as you can see we do have the programs you are looking for, as well as some advanced programs you can move up to, and the help of a nutritionist to help you achieve all of your goals. Can we begin scheduling a membership program for you today?"*

Once you have demonstrated that you can fulfill the client's needs, you make a presumptive close and ask for his business.

What if the customer is not ready? Ask them directly what it is that you need to demonstrate to welcome him as a member. Be polite.

"Mr. Tetley, when you let me know how I can accommodate you, I'll do my best to fulfill your needs. We appreciate your time, and are willing to work with you."

Move forward, but never push. A hard-sell pitch will probably create resentment and eliminate any chance you'll have to make a follow-up presentation. Some people simply need a little time to think before making a commitment, so don't burn your bridges. If you don't get the sale – make certain you part as friends.

Sales is at the heart of your operation. You need well-trained and convivial salespeople who are as ready and willing to pick up a phone and make a call as they are to open the door and take an order. Salesmanship is a skill and a craft, not a born ability. Like management and yoga skills, sales skills are developed through experience.

The Post Sale. A sale is not the end of a process; it is the beginning. You now have a relationship with the client, and like all relationships it requires some nourishing. After the sale, take the member on a detailed tour of the facility and make introductions. Set up meetings with an instructor, nutritionist or whoever is available. Care for them as you would a friend, make them feel at home and as a welcomed part of the family – your future depends on it.

Another way to say this is, don't treat the sale like a conquest. If you do, your prospective customers are likely to try and escape at some point.

There are two schools of thought on the compensation

of salespeople: salary or base pay plus commission. Ideally, you could hire a motivated salesperson who spends all working hours trying to get students for you. They would be pleasant, clean and care about the client afterward. The reality is that incentives are what get things done, and sales people require some sort of an incentive program. You need to balance an incentive program with a base pay so that your salespeople are not pushing too hard for the sale, but are doing everything you want them to do as part of the sales-and-intake process. If you don't manage the program, and follow-up on the progress, your salespeople will treat each new client as a conquest and move on to the next sale.

The post-sale is the most important part of the sale. There are many caravans and many knowledgeable caravan masters. Travelers are looking for a caravan with a master that looks out for its members.

The Language of Sales. The language of sales is precise and takes time to master. The reason so many entrepreneurs are good at sales is no mystery. They have awesome product knowledge, enthusiasm and an innate ability to see how their product or service will benefit a potential client.

A professional salesperson must first gather product knowledge. Sales are rare if the salespeople don't display an in-depth knowledge of their product. Not only must they know the product, they need to know how to describe it in an enthusiastic way. Salespeople must, every so often, sit on the other side of the counter and listen to the sales presentation, I also recommend that other professional salespeople come and hear the presentation. This helps all of you keep an objective view of the information you're offering and a chance to improve the presentation.

Pepper your presentation with statements that the prospective clients will agree with. This will help get them into an agreeable position, so that they say yes when you ask them to become a member or sign up for classes.

On the other side of agreeable statements are negative statements – they must be avoided, even in your grammar. A negative command must be followed by a negative thought. For example, "Don't think of polar bears." Now all you can think about is polar bears. "Don't come late," all you can think about is being late. "Don't worry," will make you start worrying. It's always better to communicate in the positive. For example, "Please be on time" or "Be happy!" Communicate in the positive and avoid the negative.

Surveying Current Customers. This is a must. You need unbiased feedback from customers if you are ever going to learn what wants and needs are being unfulfilled. All surveys must be blind, meaning that you do not know who sent you the comments. Some of the questions you need to ask will deal with the perception of value and others about the facility and staff. All surveys should have an open comments section where the respondent can say anything they want. Design your survey with your staff, one or two outside people, and potential customers to get the right balance of information.

There are several methods of conducting a survey.

You could mail the survey to members and include a return envelope, or you could mail the survey and ask clients to drop them off when at the studio. What is the difference between the two? A survey that is mailed back can include current and past clients, while a survey that has to be dropped off will only give you a response from those currently attending. Any survey for comments at the front desk will get a lot of gripes. A suggestion box is just as good as anything else to deal with gripes.

It is very important to get feedback from clients who have discontinued using your services. You need to know why you didn't retain them as a client. You cannot please everyone, but you need to know if there are any common concerns among those who have left so that you can address their issues.

Interpreting Survey Results. Consistent responses in any area mean you are either getting it perfect or getting it wrong. What is more often the case is mixed results. For example, if on a scale of 1 to 10 half of the answers center around 9 and half center around 2, this shows that you have very divergent expectations in that area. You may need to look at your services and offer two different memberships or service packages to accommodate these different groups.

Personal Information. You may need to collect personal information from clients for internal processing, insurance liability, regulatory or other reasons depending upon the studio and the focus of your programs. Personal information may be medical, banking or simply contact information. Any personal information you collect is private and should always protected. Information about clients should be available on a need-to-know basis only – and this applies to both instructors and staff. If the records are physical, lock them up. If they are on a computer, at a minimum, password protect them and keep access to the data limited and change the password every so often. Always set up an off-site data back up.

Pricing. If you give your services away, no one will value them. If you charge too much, no one will buy them. You must present services that are affordable and have a perceived value. Oftentimes perceived value is accomplished by studios doubling the rate they actually expect to collect, and then selling memberships at 50% during sales promotions – or offering two-for-one discounts – or, pay six months get the second six months free. You get the idea. As simple as these types of promotions sound, they do instill a perceived value in the minds of buyers. In any case, investigate what your competitors are charging, and keep your prices competitive until you've developed a reputation that supports above-market rates.

My suggestion is to offer aggressive promotional pricing when you open. This aggressive pricing is called market penetration pricing. Once you have penetrated the market, you can begin to raise your rates. I also suggest that every price increase coincide with changes in the studio. A price increase with no change in services is just a price increase. A price increase tied to changes in the studio is a price that reflects the changing value of your services. So, if you open today, and you plan to add the services of a nutritionist in the next three months, schedule your price increase to coincide with this change.

You also need to be aware of inflation. Your studio prices need to keep pace with the economy. Historically, this has averaged about 4%. Your income might be the first indicator of inflationary costs, but you shouldn't wait for changes in the economy to show up on your bottom line. You need to monitor your costs and be making changes that ensure that you don't bear the full brunt of a shifting economy. To stay even, you need to raise your prices to account for inflation or risk falling behind. At a minimum, adjust your prices each year in accordance with changes in the CPI – Consumer Price Index. Higher rates of inflation may require price increase more often than annual.

Co-Promoting. There are going to be a number of opportunities to co-promote your services, for example: attending health festivals, and working with nutritionists, product suppliers, chefs, local health food stores and other tangential services. Your studio will grow with name recognition, and to get name recognition you must continually be out in the community. Co-promoting is a way to stretch your marketing dollars because you're only paying a share of the costs to attract an audience.

What you want to avoid are promotions that will feature your direct competitors. You should be the only yoga studio in a co-promotion. It is every competitor's instinct to begin comparing their studios, and to put themselves at the top. Curb this instinct. It's better to promote yoga than just promote yourself. If you simply promote yoga, you're taking the high road, and people will understand this.

The Things We Do for Free. You have arrived here though a long journey. It's not easy to compare one journey with another, let alone describe the journey. You are a seeker. You want – no that's not strong enough – you are compelled to make a difference. While profit supports the body, making a difference nourishes the soul.

When we donate time, we will often be working with students at rehabilitation centers, senior centers, obesity clinics, stress disorders clinics, burn wards, chronic pain clinics and others. I get it. But when you do these things, see if you can offer these services through a nonprofit sponsor, so that at least you can get tax recognition for the hours you donate. Also look for additional recognition which will in turn help support your studio.

night's warm exhaled breath on the neck
walls, rocks, ground radiating heat's maw
no cooling, hair itches, skin crawls

wind waits with no direction
crimson the mornings light upon
red sea, blue sky, white wispy clouds working

sun so bright its humming
insect to beast - restless
wisps building mighty waves

scents are different,
they are faint but rich
light energy throbbing

camel saddles creak
all beasts facing west
backs are to the storm

haboob's towering tide
the angry red waves crash
oasis beasts seek shelter

sand sizzles across palm fronds
dunes dusty shimmering
rich scents now of earth

muddy blobs plop in the clear stream
squalls glue red mud to everything
torrents scrub red sea from all

wind slackens with no direction
steam rises from a quenched fire
after cooling, inhaling rich scents

Mister sent out 7 camels with provisions for the caravan. They will camp after 5 days ride in the red wadi and wait. Bandits are 2 days ride from the oasis laden with some spoils. They be lazy now or not. If bandits take the caravan's provisions, the caravan would have to drop cargo and return to the oasis. If the bandits rob the advance camels - they will be satiated and return to their villages.

Mister does not know what may be - bandit attacks. Mister knows provisions are required for the desert past the red wadi.

10 Management by Objectives

It is impossible to prepare you for the use of management by objectives in a few short paragraphs. But I would like to use it to introduce the subject. Management By Objectives, or MBO, as it is affectionately called, is a concept popularized by Peter Drucker more than 50 years ago. This is a strategy for managing people that focuses on their ability to complete individual and team goals. MBO has been widely implemented in large and small organizations since its inception by Drucker in his book *"The Practice of Management"*.

Management is about establishing objectives while communicating and developing a dialogue among all people and entities responsible for accomplishing the stated objectives. A successful manager will attempt to align the employees' goals with the goals of the organization. This ensures that everyone is clear about what should be done, what their role is, and how their performance benefits the goals of the entire organization.

In defining the tools used in management by objective, proponents created an alphabet soup of acronyms. MBO tools are goals, objectives, action steps, SMART Goals, objectives and action steps, SWOT assessment, and measuring progress with KRAs. A definition of terms will get us a lot closer to understanding the theory.

The first step in MBO is to clearly explain to your staff what it is you're doing and why you're doing it. The second step is defining the actual objectives you expect to realize, and how you intend to measure your success.

This can be challenging in its own right, as you seek to find a balance between too much information and the information necessary to realize specific goals.

MBO is meant to help employees assess and prioritize their efforts to make certain those efforts are focused on the bottom line and organizational values. The process also helps your team understand what behaviors the organization doesn't value, and what activities may not be contributing to your objectives.

Good intentions are no substitute for organization and leadership, for accountability, performance and results.

The purpose of an organization is to enable common men to do uncommon things.

One is responsible for one's impacts, whether they are intended or not.

Tell me what you are going to do on Monday that is different.

Peter Drucker 1909 - 1995

An example of a negative behavior is the activity trap. This is seen when people get so busy doing things that they forget to ask whether the things they're doing are the right things. This is an important concept for everyone in an organization to understand. MBO is designed to help you avoid activity traps by helping your employees understand their goals and making the work that they do more structured toward accomplishing the organization's goals.

SMART Objectives are:

$$S = Specific$$
$$M = Measurable$$
$$A = Achievable$$
$$R = Realistic$$
$$T = Timed$$

SMART defines several factors that should be present in your objectives in order for them to be effective.

First, they should be specific. In other words, they should specifically describe the result that is desired.
In order to be able to use any objective as a part of a review process it needs to be very clear and measurable, so everyone can see if a person has met the objective or not.

The objectives must be achievable. For instance, an objective that requires "100 percent customer satisfaction" isn't realistically achievable. It's not realistic to expect that outsiders will be 100 percent satisfied with any performance.

Realistic objectives are objectives that recognize some factors cannot be controlled. Said another way, realistic goals are potentially challenging but not so challenging that they cannot succeed. You can only control what you have the power to influence – you cannot control the weather, or actions of third parties not related to your enterprise.

The final factor for a good objective is that it is based on time. This is the key anchor in making the objective real and tangible. A time period is identified for completion, and the employee or group will be held accountable for the successful completion of the objective.

Key Result Areas (KRAs) are what you measure to determine your success in accomplishing your objectives. KRAs identify:

- The major metrics to success in a job.
- Critical subjects for the target period.
- Areas in which a manager must achieve results to be most successful.
- Critical make-or-break areas of a job function.
- High priority matters for success during the target period.

An example of a KRA for your studio could be:

1) number of new inquires per week
2) conversion of new inquires to memberships
3) membership-renewal rate
4) customer satisfaction
5) gross revenue per:
   a) square feet
   b) instructor
   c) member

The most important and valuable purpose of KRAs is to help the manager direct his limited time and resources (time, money, people, plant and equipment) to the most important metrics, those that actually identify success, and where effort to improve will provide the greatest returns.

A SWOT analysis identifies:

S = Strengths
W = Weaknesses
O = Opportunities
T = Threats

A SWOT analysis is completed on each KRA – thus a manager who has seven KRAs will have seven different SWOT analysis sheets.

A SWOT analysis is used to provide input as you create strategies. You will add information to the SWOT analysis by asking the following four questions and incorporating your answers into future strategies:

- How can we capitalize on our strengths?
- How can we compensate for our weaknesses?
- How can we exploit and benefit from our opportunities?
- How can we mitigate threats?

Ideally a team that represents a broad range of perspectives should be assembled to carry out a SWOT analysis. Assemble people from every department in the organization when doing a SWOT analysis – and include people from outside the organization if they can offer constructive advice. Use all of the key people you can assemble to help you with your analysis.

MBO is about making changes that will add information to, and accelerate the performance of your organization. Your desire is to cultivate growth and efficiencies that will differentiate your organization from others with less information and inferior management.

As already stated, MBO is an effort to align the employees' goals with the goals of the organization. These efforts can be defeated by such subtle oversights as poorly defined job descriptions. A bad job description is focused on tasks, separation of duties, and is generally territorial in nature. A good job description deals with job-related functions along with the objectives of the employee, the division, the field of endeavor and the enterprise. The good job description is designed to align the employee's goals with the goals of the organization.

A Summary of the Process

- Objectives are a clear set of results planned for. The objectives must be SMART.

    SMART = Specific, Measurable, Achievable, Realistic, Timed

- Action Steps are the steps needed, in aggregate, to accomplish an objective. It is literally identifing the actions necessary to achieve your objective. Action steps are a day-to-day plan for managing change.
- Goal-setting involves establishing a specific set or sets of measurable and time-targeted objectives
- Achieving a goal is what occurs when all of the objectives have been realized.Objectives are reached as a result of the completion of a number of action steps.

How it Fails

- Decrees are sent from on high as opposed to bi-level negotiations.
- A lack of commitment from senior management.
- An inability to develop organization goals and objectives.
- A lack of accountability from participants.
- Failure to follow-up.
- Failure to evaluate performance.
- Lack of flexibility.
- Lack of time.

This is a powerful management tool, the most real and authentic I have come across. The process is not difficult, but it will not happen without a focused effort. The challenge is to constructively change what you do every day, and make a habit of following the plan. This is an open process that identifies the goals of the organization for everyone to see. This is a process that gets people out of their pigeonholes and gets them to serve the organizational needs rather than to defend their territory. It is a dynamic process that needs to be reviewed, modified and reviewed again in light of your successes. If you choose to follow this process, you choose to succeed.

I urge you to explore the MBO concept, and, if you are enthusiastic enough, read *Management: Tasks, Responsibilities, Practices*, also by Drucker.

As in all things, you will get better with practice. Use these tools for everything from managing your enterprise to working around the house.

Intentional direction drives the caravan to arrive at its destination in discreet, objective steps, oasis by oasis, rest by rest, with driving action steps guiding each day of the journey. Detours in the desert increase the chance of banditry and death.

11 Financing

A well-written business plan will do two things. It will define your capital requirements, and it will reveal a project timeline to recover the investment and reach a point of profitability. If you need to borrow money, the business plan will be the focal point of the lender or investor – and the soundness of the plan will determine their interest in the plan. Do your homework.

A lender's job is to rip your plan apart. "You forgot to include costs for A, B and C..." "Why are you including costs for X, Y and Z?" "You can't hire that kind of help for that money." Lenders work with rule-of-thumb numbers. Their job is to understand what things cost, and to give your business plan a reality check. They have a rough idea of what it costs to make a space habitable using a fixed cost and a 100-square-foot cost. They also understand hiring, employee, advertising and promotional costs. These are people who have "been there and done that." They're going to look at all of your numbers and subject them to a reality check. The more research you do for your plan, the more comprehensive you make it, so it realistically addresses revenues and expenses, the more likely you are to find a financial partner. There are few things more satisfying than to respond to an investor's inquiries with solid documentation and letters of commitment or understanding.

If you're going to a conventional lending source, chances are you will have to mortgage your house, and they will have little interest in your business plan. What they want is to be fully secured by your equity. If you're looking for a real financial partner, you're going to have to look at some unconventional sources of funding. These investors are going to be very interested in your plan, and when they loan money they do indeed foresee themselves as partners.

Most unconventional lenders have a limited area of expertise; so don't be upset if you get turned down. Every time you present your plan you're going to get some insight into the perceived strengths and weaknesses of it. You don't necessarily have to try and incorporate all of the suggestions you get from investors into your plan – but if the suggestions make sense to you, or you've heard them a couple of times, you should consider recasting your plan. In reality, a lot of these investors are fools. Many professional investors, who either didn't understand or didn't agree with the vision, turned Bill Gates away. Don't let it get you down.

You need to have and use the correct resources to make the journey and establish your studio. If you anticipate that you'll have plenty of students in 11 months, and thus only funds for 11 months – you risk the vagaries of an uncertain market and running out of funds too early. Fund for 24 months, and you risk having a bustling studio and too many partners you did not need. By studying the past, you can come to many conclusions about the future that are wrong. You cannot come to conclusions about what has not yet happened – you can only have a framework within which you can measure your experiences.

We are all welcomed as guests at the oasis, for that is the law of the traveler and the host. But, because you are invited in, do not think that you are permitted to be a burden. Resources are scarce, and everyone coming to and from the oasis is living on the edge. Make a mistake in the caravan, and people die. Make a mistake at the oasis, and it may return to the desert. People are sent out into the desert when they become a burden at the oasis. People are killed for taking water from wells that do not belong to them. Expectations matter to all involved, and they must be clearly communicated. Failed expectations are the root of all conflict. Most conflict involves scarce resources. Your scarce resources are time and money.

Banking. You must keep all of your business transactions separate from your personal finances. All of your personal money put into the business should be in the form of a loan that is fully documented, pays you interest, includes terms for default and has a date specific for repayment. This will require separate bank accounts. Assuming you're going to have a payroll, you should set up a separate account strictly for payroll. When choosing a bank, make sure that you select a bank that can offer you all of the merchant services you're going to require. If you can solve all of your banking issues with a single bank, life will be a lot easier.

We assume you're familiar with how checking accounts work, but you may not be as familiar with how credit cards work. In order to offer services in the modern world, there's simply no way that you can succeed without accepting credit cards for payment. Accepting credit cards also allows you to automatically charge periodic dues if you have a membership contract on file, so you will need to check on software features available to you when selecting a provider.

In order to accept credit cards you need two things, a merchant account and a service provider. Your bank will create the merchant account, and will either be your service provider, or direct you to independent service providers that work with your bank . The fees for setting up an account shouldn't exceed $200 to $300, not including any point-of-sale (POS) equipment. The POS equipment, the card swipe equipment, can either be purchased or leased on a monthly basis. I would recommend a purchase, as there is equipment on the market beginning at around $100. You can buy POS software for a PC for well under $100, and simply add a keyboard with a swipe function.

Your cost for settling transactions will have two components, a fixed fee for every transaction and a percentage fee. A reasonable range for the fixed transaction fee is 18 to 25 cents, and 2% to 3% for the percentage fee. For example, if your fees are 20 cents plus 2.5%, on a $10 charge you would pay 0.20 + 0.25 = 45 cents, and on a $100 charge you would pay 0.20 + 2.50 = $2.70.

When a charge is completed, the service provider will transfer the funds to your merchant account. How timely the funds are transferred will depend on the provider, a few will transfer funds in real time, others overnight, and some will take two to five days.

The caravan travels on its stomach. Travelers and the camels must be fed along the way. There is a trade-off on how much food you carry when traveling. You may be able to find sufficient fodder for the camels along the way, or not. Too little food, and you must rely upon merchants along the way to sell you more – but they will sell it dear. Too much, and you limit cargo. You require knowledge of the road you are going to travel. You will ask all travelers inbound about the nature of their caravan and their experiences. You use their experiences to craft you expectation. Knowing the limits of their information is valuable. The inbound information is last month's information and is stale or it may be meant to deceive you into taking a route near bandits. Timing and Tellers of information color the information. Just imagine the experience of a journey in early April – where winter conditions are possible – versus late May when the heat may already be intense. Less than 60 days can make a big difference.

12 Opening the Doors

You need to exploit your Grand Opening as long as you can. It's not unusual to be open 30 to 60 days prior to the official Grand Opening. This gives you an opportunity to meet with the press and work out the bugs in the operation. No matter how careful a planner you may be, you will have problems.

When the day comes you need to have a media blast and get as much information out to the public as you can. Some cheesy examples are, get the mayor of the city to cut the ribbon at an opening ceremony, such elected officials bring the media in tow. Send out press releases to all of the media, but be especially solicitous of the local newspapers – printed and Internet, that cover your demographic area – invite media in for a trial session. This is also a time for massive couponing and co-promotions to symbiotic business such as health food stores, nutrition centers and anyone one else you can think of. Petition the city signage office workers to allow you to have a huge "Grand Opening" banner on the side of the building for 30 to 60 days. Mine all of your contacts and all of the contacts of your instructors as well as students to get names and address for invitations to the grand opening. The party should last four to eight weeks. It is the one and only grand opening you will ever have – so keep the party rolling as long as you can.

Continuing Operations. Every studio is different. As you begin to run the studio, write down everything you tell staff in a private log. Those things that you find yourself repeating may need to go into an operations manual. This private log will be the kernel of understanding your operations and what works and especially what does not work so future staff and managers do not repeat errors.

You need to have a system of checks and balances when taking in money and possessing inventory for sale. Employees and the public will steal from you. All you can do is to make the opportunity as rare as you can.

One day you are going to need to take a vacation – a real one. Begin by taking one-day vacations and finding out what goes wrong while you are gone. Tell staff you are leaving for two days and come back early the second day and surprise them – if they act shocked – you need to figure out what they were doing when they expected you to be away.

It is very reasonable and inexpensive to have concealed video surveillance over the cash register and the merchandise. It is also important to have some sort of fool-resistant time clock to monitor hourly employees and the coming and going of instructors. It will only take a few days of operation before you get the problems.

There are many different solutions – but that is another book and would make no sense until you have run the business for a while. When you feel the business can run without you and you have tested it a few times – take the vacation with family and relax.

The Value of My Business. You've built your own business, you've made a profit, and you've had fun. But some day it will end, and how it ends is something you should be thinking about now. Most people, when they go into business for themselves either buy an existing business, or buy a franchise. Only the most ambitious actually create a new business model and make it work.

If you want your enterprise to survive you, you need to think about planning for the continuity of the enterprise. Whether it's because you want to change your line of work, you retire, you die, or you move to a new location, a plan has to be in place for the business to survive. Planning for the continuity of your business without your participation is referred to as an exit strategy. Generally, small businesses are sold through a business broker to an employee or to a family member.

Here are some of the issues you will encounter in transitioning a business, issues that you can begin addressing even as you start your business.

> Operations Manual. One of the many reasons people buy franchises is to get the operations manual. The manual will provide them an answer for any question they are likely to encounter. A franchise is simply a clone of an existing business, and the people who made the existing business successful have detailed how they made it work, what can go wrong, and where the land mines are. Some of these manuals are so detailed that they specify what wattage of lighting should be in the rest rooms. You not only need to create a manual, but update it continually. It can be as simple as a single document on your computer with

various topics followed by your notes on those topics. Add topics and comments freely as you stumble upon new information and face new crises. What software are you using to manage your business, and why? What features are you using? What information is collected? What tools are used for prospecting, and where is the information kept? Which employees have access to what databases? Who are your suppliers? What purchasing choices are important to your success, and what are some of the mistakes you've made in purchasing? Which employees are authorized to make purchases, what are the limits of their authority, and what are the procedures for monitoring purchases? The operations manual should be complete enough that, in your absence, a new manager could take over with minimal interruption to the business.

Key employees. If a business depends upon the enterprise-specific knowledge of key employees, it is unlikely to survive their departure. While almost all skills can be replaced, if only one person knows the passwords to the operating software, or knows how to deliver services in the manner the clientele expect, there are going to be costly disruptions when that person leaves. Specific information on your clients, their individual needs, and any customer support issues, should all be tracked in a database that's easily accessible. And, of course, the structure of this database should be detailed in the operations manual.

Valuation and Financing. If you have made the

enterprise profitable, and are trying to sell it, you and the buyer are going to have to address the issues of valuation and financing. The more profitable the business is, the higher the selling price is going to be. As you're beginning the business, finding financing is going to be based upon your experience, your business plan and your personal investment. The only information the lender has is your plan to proceed and your projections about how the plan will pay off. When you sell your business, the buyer will have an empirical record of the earning capabilities of the enterprise. It's much easier for the buyer of an established business to get financing, assuming the business has been valued correctly. The topic of business valuation is far too complicated to be addressed adequately here, but suffice it to say that every dollar that you can add to the bottom line will come back to you in multiples when you sell the business. To that end, begin your business with good accounting practices and an accountant to audit your records and advise you. A good set of books and a history of good record-keeping practices will serve you well when you decide to sell your business.

Franchising / Licensing. There may come a time when your business is successful enough that you are approached with requests to franchise or license your name. This is when you can pat yourself on the back for having your trade name and artwork trademarked. This is also a time when you'll be glad you put a little extra effort into maintaining an up-to-date and comprehensive operations manual. Franchising and licensing are an excellent opportunity for you to make money and strengthen your brand. The buyer gets to clone your operation, including the literature, marketing materials, software setup, artwork and signage. The buyer also gets the benefit of a name that has already been branded, and a proven track record of earnings. Both strategies are potential win-win arrangements, but there are some potential issues you need to be aware of.

Franchising has it's own set of laws, while licensing is a form of contract law. The difference between the two is night and day, both in the time necessary to implement and the legal costs associated with structuring compliance. While we're all familiar with franchising as a concept, you should think about licensing as a means of expanding your business if the subject comes up. The differences are subtle, but important. You will need to retain a good lawyer experienced in franchising and licensing law if you intend to expand in this manner.

Suggested Topics to Include in Your Business Plan

Summary. A summary, often referred to as an executive summary, should be the first page of your plan. It should not be more than a single page in length, and is better if kept to two or three paragraphs. It should concisely explain the business concept, where you are currently in your plans, what assets you bring to the venture, and your financial needs. People who invest in business opportunities may review a dozen or more plans a day, and invest in one per month. The summary is about as far as they will get in most plans. This is the hook – this is where you want to get the reader's attention – make it good.

Market Research. Include your analysis of the market you intend to serve, how that market has evolved, and where you believe it is headed. Include, and reference, all source materials you have used in reaching your conclusions. Define the estimated size and demographic of your target customers, and what their needs are.

Competitive Analysis. Include your research on who is currently serving your target market, what they are providing, and what they are charging. Add information about trends in the field, and what services are being offered in other markets as well as how they're being sold. In your competitive analysis you should describe any opportunities that you feel exist, as well as any threats to your business plan. It is critically important to investors that you have studied and researched the risks involved in your own plan – do not ignore this part of the written plan.

Strategy. Define each of the critical steps that are going to make your plan unfold as it was designed. Summarize both your competitive capabilities and your competitive weaknesses. Explain how you are going to overcome your weaknesses. This is a good place to discuss your

SWOT analysis and your approach to business management.

Products and Services. Here, include a brief description of every income source that is mentioned in your plan. Describe how everything is priced, and how those prices compare to similar services being offered in your market. Describe the assumptions that you used to calculate your revenue selling these products and services.

Marketing and Sales. In this section you need to summarize your marketing strategy. Will you be using direct mailing, handouts or print advertising? Describe how you're acquiring mailing lists, what they cost, how the names were qualified and chosen, where handouts will be distributed and by whom, what publications you intend to advertise in as well as their reader profile, circulation and prices. Also describe what assumptions you are making about the effectiveness of the advertising. Describe how you will sell your services to prospective clients. Discuss pricing issues, the market, your personal philosophy, and how you set prices for the first year. Include information about promotions you intend to sponsor, incentives you will use to move your sales efforts forward, and include the cost of these programs.

Operations. Include a short biography of people who you know will be involved in the venture, making sure to include their experience as it relates to the position they will hold in your organization. Define the structure of the management team and where you intend to recruit the talent that has not yet been identified. Describe the facilities that have already been identified, along with all costs, or define the features needed in a property and describe all of your assumptions about cost. Describe what customer support services you intend to offer, and who or what position will be responsible for dealing with customers.

Financials. The spreadsheets we worked on earlier are the real business plan – the rest of it is the narrative. You do need to do both if you are using the plan to raise money, but in either case, the financials are done first. The spreadsheet is where you begin making your assumptions and inserting hard data as you uncover it. Make sure that every assumption in the financial model is described somewhere in the narrative, and that your description includes a basis for the assumption. The basis for some of your assumptions may simply be a best guess from information you've discovered in your research. Financial professionals understand terms such as organic growth, because they understand that there will always be some number of people who simply stumble upon your business. What you need to describe is how you chose your rate of organic growth. If you are in an industrial park, the rate is going to be very close to zero, and if you're in a high-traffic shopping mall you're expecting your organic growth rate to be quite high. You need to add some meat to your assumptions, offer information, and describe a process that would lead reasonable people to come to the same conclusions that you did. If you can't lead reasonable people to adopt your assumptions, you need to rethink your assumptions.

Pop Page Quiz

Following the last model for the business plan that was added to the text, we have been discussing several operational issues. If you read carefully, many of the topics that were covered presented suggestions, and associated expenses, that were not addressed in the business plan. Did you notice?

See if you can figure out how to update the business plan to reflect the new expenses we've identified in the narrative. My list is on the following page for updating your model business plan.

Added Expenses

I don't expect that our lists will match, but I noticed that the following expenses that are in the narrative business plan were not adequately addressed in the business plan model:

- A budget for help wanted advertisements.
- Private background checks for new employees.
- Printing of employee manuals, operating manuals and records storage.
- Computers and database for operations.
- Uniforms.
- Insurance.
- Contact management / sales software.
- Credit transaction fees.
- POS terminal.
- Ongoing accounting and auditing services.

The Mister Says . . .

The camel-pullers are working in their ba and are loading the camels. It is but hours to departure. The air is still, cool and sweet.

The first-time camel-pullers are having visions of their distant destination.

For the camels-pullers that have their own lian, it is of the process of the coming journey that occupies their thoughts. Is the ratio of food to cargo correct for the distance? Have the camels all been checked and rechecked, to ensure they will survive the journey and not die with their load in the desert? Is my counterpart of the ba able and reliable?

The Mister is concerned with information that has come in from the inbound caravans, listening to the tales of the journey and conditions of the routes to be chosen – balancing safety and speed and the color of their tales. The mountain route is quick, but it is early spring and will provide little fodder but good water. The valley route has good fodder and water, but there are many others that will travel this way who may consume the fodder and foul the water. Mister is paid for the journey by fees and a share of the cargo. What is the best balance? He eyes the camel-pullers and the ba pairs – already there are words of frustration. Will the ba last the journey, or will he have to intervene? Will family honor be defended and feuds avenged on the journey – and what should Mister's reaction be? Can he find an experienced camel puller to train? What of the raiders? What is the knowledge of his activity, and who in the oasis is informing the raiders of the plans of the caravans? Does he tell of his decisions, or does he misdirect? Mister keeps his own confidence.

The more patient you become, the more you learn. The more you learn the greater the responsibilities you take on. The greater the responsibilities you assume, the more fulfilling but lonelier the journey becomes.

The camels are loaded, the lians are ready. It is time to go. As you leave the oasis, you feel the heat you will battle throughout the journey, and taste the dust. You are at ease. You are confident in your preparations.

Additional Material

There are several spreadsheets scattered in the text. We have provided downloads for you to use at www.yogaforprofit.com

Please read several different ways to write your business plan - not all are good, but all are better than none.

Please read Peter Drucker's book, *"The Practice of Management"*.

Always seek competent legal and accounting advice. Not all lawyers and accountants are equal, look for someone who specializes in small businesses as clients.

If you wish some additional help, please consider calling us at (480) 838-1728 for telephonic business consulting.

A blessed night is the reward for the day. Dawn's peace is night's reward.